Anne Phillips

Our Bodies, Whose Property?

Princeton University Press

Princeton and Oxford

Library of Congress Cataloging-in-Publication Data

Phillips, Anne, 1950-
   Our bodies, whose property? / Anne Phillips.
    pages cm
   Summary: "No one wants to be treated like an object, regarded as an item of
property, or put up for sale. Yet many people frame personal autonomy in terms
of self-ownership, representing themselves as property owners with the right to
do as they wish with their bodies. Others do not use the language of property,
but are similarly insistent on the rights of free individuals to decide for themselves whether to engage in commercial transactions for sex, reproduction, or
organ sales. Drawing on analyses of rape, surrogacy, and markets in human
organs, Our Bodies, Whose Property? challenges notions of freedom based
on ownership of our bodies and argues against the normalization of markets
in bodily services and parts. Anne Phillips explores the risks associated with
metaphors of property and the reasons why the commodification of the body
remains problematic. What, she asks, is wrong with thinking of oneself as the
owner of one's body? What is wrong with making our bodies available for rent
or sale? What, if anything, is the difference between markets in sex, reproduction, or human body parts, and the other markets we commonly applaud?
Phillips contends that body markets occupy the outer edges of a continuum
that is, in some way, a feature of all labor markets. But she also emphasizes
that we all have bodies, and considers the implications of this otherwise banal
fact for equality. Bodies remind us of shared vulnerability, alerting us to the
common experience of living as embodied beings in the same world. Examin-
ing the complex issue of body exceptionalism, Our Bodies, Whose Property?
demonstrates that treating the body as property makes human equality harder
to comprehend"—Provided by publisher.
   Includes bibliographical references and index.
   ISBN 978-0-691-15086-4 (hardback)
   1. Liberty. 2. Capitalism. 3. Human body. 4. Property. I. Title.
   JC585.P444 2013
   323.44—dc23   2012046764

British Library Cataloging-in-Publication Data is available

Contents

Acknowledgements

MY BIGGEST DEBT, IN WRITING this book, is to my students, and particularly those who took my course in Feminist Political Theory as part of their MSc programme at the London School of Economics. In our often finely balanced debates about prostitution and surrogacy, I developed and clarified many of the thoughts that appear in this book. I also gradually overcame my initial preference, which was to declare these difficult issues and sit on the fence.

I wrote one of the chapters while holding a visiting fellowship at the Australian National University in February–April 2009. The invitation came courtesy of John Dryzek, who had expected me to work on matters of democracy but tolerantly accepted me writing about bodies instead. I presented versions of various chapters at philosophy, gender, and political theory seminars at the Universities of Sydney, Amsterdam, Oxford, and Cambridge, at the Victoria University of Wellington, and the London School of Economics, and benefitted from a good deal of critical feedback. Some of the argument had an early outing in an essay, "'It's My Body and I'll Do What I Like with It': Bodies as Objects and Property," published in *Political Theory* (39, no. 6 [2011]: 724–48). I am grateful to the publishers for permission to reproduce parts of that essay here. I am even more grateful to the editors and readers for Princeton University Press and *Political Theory*, who took me to task on various oddities and helped me tighten the argument. Colleagues in my two departments—the Gender Institute and the Department of Government—gave me pause for thought on many occasions, as did Ciaran Driver, partner of many infuriating discussions, who tried to curb my excesses as regards both property and the market. My thanks to all.

**Our Bodies,
Whose Property?**

Introduction

THIS IS A BOOK ABOUT MARKETS, bodies, and property. It considers what, if anything, is the difference between markets in sex or reproduction or human body parts and the other markets we commonly applaud. What—if anything—makes the body special? People otherwise untroubled by the workings of market society often oppose commercial transactions in what we might call intimate bodily services or body products and parts. But can we justify what Nir Eyal terms "body exceptionalism"?[1] Or is thinking the body special a kind of sentimentalism that blocks clear thinking about matters such as prostitution, surrogate motherhood, and the sale of spare kidneys?

In exploring these questions, I continue arguments opened up in a number of recent contributions, including Margaret Radin's *Contested Commodities*, Debra Satz's *Why Some Things Should Not Be For Sale*, and Michael Sandel's *What Money Can't Buy*.[2] I share with all three of these the view that some things should not be for sale, and that it is not transparently obvious either why this is so or which these are. I share with the first two a feminist-inflected focus on the body. I consider, however, not just markets and the body, for I am also concerned with the implications and consequences of thinking of the body as something that we own. I examine cases of body commodification, focusing on commercial surrogacy and markets in body parts, but I also consider instances where thinking of the body as property has no obvious implications in terms of making it available for sale. My main example of this latter is what happens to our understanding of rape when the body is conceived as property and rape as a property crime. Thinking of the body as property potentially minimises its significance to our sense of who we are, and in many contexts accustoms us to thinking of it as a marketable resource. There is, however, no inevitable line of determination between adopting the metaphors of property and sending the body to market, and there is some evidence— discussed later—that those engaged in body trades resist the language of property. The book addresses, therefore, two distinct though related questions. What, if anything, is wrong with thinking of oneself as the owner of one's body? What, if anything, is wrong with making our bodies available for rent or sale?

There is currently an international consensus that bodies are *not* property, and that neither human bodies nor human body parts should be traded as commodities. Slave markets are repudiated in every country in the world, though not entirely eliminated. Markets in babies are also illegal, though in academic debate at least, they not so entirely repudiated.[3] Marriage markets are challenged by a variety of human rights conventions that stress the rights of individuals to determine for themselves when and whom they marry. In these instances, what is being banned is the trade in *someone else's* body, but governments around the world also ban trading in one's own. That the kidney or cornea is yours (it clearly isn't anyone else's) is regarded as beside the point, and while there is a thriving global market in live human organs,[4] this is almost entirely illegal. Sales of human gametes are legal in some countries but banned in others. Regulation of prostitution and commercial surrogacy[5] also varies, with some jurisdictions treating both as illegal, others criminalising one but not the other, and others still treating both as legitimate markets. Even allowing for these variations, there is clearly a perception that the body being yours is not enough to legitimate its trade. The body *is* yours, but that does not make it property, and does not give you the automatic right to determine whether to rent out or sell.

Why not? What justifies these restrictions on free individuals choosing to trade in their bodies and body parts? Do they depend, perhaps, on religious notions of the body that cannot now—indeed never could—be regarded as universally shared? Can we continue, moreover, to justify the restrictions in a world where innovations in medical and reproductive technology create an ever-increasing demand? Prostitution has been with us for millennia, with arguments swirling backwards and forwards as to whether it should be legal, but it is now joined by more widely approved activities, where the burning issue is not so much whether they should be permitted, but whether they should be traded and paid. In vitro fertilisation has opened up unanticipated opportunities for the infertile to deploy someone else's body to carry an embryo to full term: most countries permit "altruistic" surrogacy, but many ban its commercial form. The success of complex transplant operations has created a use for, and thereby a shortage of, human body parts: though the Catholic Church was, for a time, opposed even to altruistic donation, the donation of human organs to save and extend life is now widely approved, but not their sale. Stem cell research currently depends on supplies of human ova: here, there is considerable opposition even to the research, but the difficult additional question is whether we should turn to the market for a steady supply of these eggs.

Developments in medical and reproductive technology have enabled many generous examples of donation: women acting as surrogates for their infertile relatives or friends, organ donors undergoing intrusive and potentially dangerous operations in order to save the lives of complete strangers, and women volunteering access to their ovaries in order to assist the infertile or further medical research. But donation falls considerably short of the demand, and a growing number of commentators argue that restrictions on body trades should be lifted and that those who wish to should be allowed (openly) to sell. In the United Kingdom in 2011, there were seven thousand patients waiting for a kidney transplant, and only one in three of these was likely to be offered the operation in time. The number willing to donate live kidneys continues to rise, but is still below a thousand (again, my figure is from the United Kingdom), and only a further fifteen hundred organs are likely to become available through the death of a donor.[6] In countries where markets in human gametes are banned, there is a similar shortfall in the supply of eggs. If monetary incentives can increase the supply—thereby enhancing and saving lives—what's wrong with introducing a market? Or as Julian Savulescu, one supporter of regulated markets in human organs, asks, "if we should be allowed to sell our labour, why not sell the means to that labour?"[7]

In the seventeenth century, we might have called on religion to answer this question. When John Locke made his classic statement about every man having "a property in his person," he did not understand this as implying that men owned their bodies, and certainly not as conveying their absolute right to do as they wished with their bodily parts.[8] It was rare in the seventeenth century to think of the self in terms of a body. If the body belonged to anyone, moreover, it belonged to God, hence the widely accepted prohibitions on suicide and self-mutilation. Although people do still call on this argument to explain why the body is special, it is no longer so generally available. We cannot so readily regard the body as God's property, or think of it, as St. Paul recommended, as "a temple of the Holy Spirit."[9]

Nor can we so readily rely on the later Marxist critique, which stressed the dangers of unbridled commodification and the alienation involved in thinking of oneself in property terms. Precisely because of that rampant commodification, many goods and activities previously regarded as outside the market are now routinely bought and sold. The fact that something used to be exempt no longer carries such weight. One might take a principled stand against the commodification of anything that has so far managed to remain outside: I confess to some unreconstructed tendency in this direction. But with the remarketisation of so much that had come to be run as public services (the selling off of state-run utilities, the privatisation of public hospitals and schools), and the commodification of so much that had been thought of as nonmarket (the commercialisation of feeling, for example, analysed in Arlie Hochschild's *The Managed Heart*[10]), it is not so obvious why the commodification of the body should fall into a category apart.

Appeals to feminism also have their problems, for while feminism provides many resources for challenging notions of the body as owned—resources I address more fully in chapter one—it also alerts us to the difficulties in singling out markets in bodies from other kinds of markets. My own arguments are framed by feminism, and while the book is not an intervention in exclusively feminist debates, my approach to markets, bodies, and property is very much shaped by feminist politics and literature. I am inspired by that literature to query the mind/body dualism that often accompanies the case for markets in bodies. The frequent feminist insistence on recognising ourselves as embodied beings also, however, discourages us from thinking that "the body" can provide a clear demarcation line telling us which things or activities are legitimately up for sale.

If all activities, including the most seemingly cerebral, involve bodies, some of what is problematic about markets in bodily services or parts is going to be present in other markets too.

Agency and Coercion

These difficulties explain, I think, why much of the critique of prostitution or the trade in human body parts has focused on coercion by people or economic circumstance, and why much of the critique of surrogacy contracts has focused on the difficulty of knowing, at the beginning of a pregnancy, how you will later feel about the requirement to relinquish a child. In current political discourse, prostitution is sometimes treated almost as synonymous with sex trafficking, as if all those who enter sex work for a living are tricked into it by lying go-betweens, or have been kidnapped and imprisoned and forced to engage in the trade. Sex trafficking and sex slavery undoubtedly exist, and I have no quarrel with national and international initiatives that enable people to escape these conditions and prosecute those responsible. (Although I would quarrel with the tendency then simply to deport the "victims.") But the blurring of boundaries between prostitution and sex trafficking, and the seeming desire to consider all sex workers as victims of trafficking, understates the agency of those who decide to work in the sex trades and makes the existence of coercion the central, perhaps even only, concern. If people are tricked or forced, then prostitution is self-evidently wrong. But what if people understand what they are letting themselves in for and take on the work in full knowledge of what it entails? Are we then left with no basis for critique?

In the illegal trade in body parts, there is also considerable trickery and deception: cases in which people wake up from a routine operation to discover that an organ has been removed without their consent, or agree to the removal of organs for transplant but under false assurances about the risks. Without exception, there is also economic coercion, for it is the coerciveness of a pressing economic need to repay a debt collector or finance a child's operation or give one's children a better start in life that leads people to this course of action. For most critics, these are the reasons for objecting to the trade: the trickery, deception, the failure to provide adequate after care to those who supply the organs, and the extreme economic need that propels them into the sale. But, again, what if we could envisage different circumstances under which all parties were fully informed of the risks, everyone had access to a decent minimum income, and yet some people still expressed their willingness to sell a spare kidney or cornea? Would there be any remaining basis for condemning this trade?

In *What Money Can't Buy*, Michael Sandel distinguishes two categories of objection to markets: the fairness objection and the corruption one. In the fairness objection—which roughly parallels what I am calling coercion—the problem is that some so-called choices are not truly voluntary, perhaps because of trickery and deception, but more often just because of background inequalities of bargaining that "coerce the disadvantaged and undermine the fairness of the deals they make."[11] People will differ in how seriously they take Sandel's objection, and the more hard-headed among us may say that all deals are made against unequal conditions, and that so long as the parties to them agree (are not tricked or deceived), they are all getting something they want. That some may get more out of the deal than others is, from this perspective, beside the point. What Sandel stresses is that the fairness objection does not exhaust all the possible problems with a market. Even if a society has established fair bargaining conditions, there can still be, he argues, some things that money should not buy. This second, corruption, objection "focuses on the character of the goods themselves and the norms that should govern them."[12] He argues that the nature of some goods is diminished, degraded, or demeaned (terms he employs extensively in the book) when they are made available for sale.

I, too, think there is more at stake than whether people are making their decisions under fair bargaining conditions, and that even contracts fairly entered into can still be problematic.[13] Choice does not legitimate everything, and the free choice of the individual cannot be our only moral touchstone.[14] Ironically, making choice the central concern may lead to a denial of people's agency, for if the only grounds on which an activity can be regarded as unacceptable is that people did not voluntarily choose it, there will be a temptation to understate the extent to which they knew what they were doing. If anything freely chosen is legitimate, then anything considered illegitimate cannot have been freely chosen: we may simply fail to recognise people as agentic individuals when what they "choose" to do falls too far outside our comprehension. This has been a problem in the analysis of prostitution, where those most critical of the practice have tended to represent sex workers as the overwhelmed victims of an all-powerful patriarchy; it has been a problem in the analysis of commercial surrogacy, where the key fallback position for those questioning the practice is that surrogate mothers cannot really know what they have agreed to until the baby is born; it is a problem in the analysis of the trade in human organs, where the vendors become faceless victims and their agency disappears. The better assumption is that everyone has agency, and that while people are more or less well informed, more or less constrained by circumstance, facing a larger or smaller set of alternatives, the vast majority of us are thinking agents who make a choice. We need, as Carol Wolkowitz puts it, to be able to distinguish between "the agency that everyone has, except in the most extreme conditions, however curtailed and constrained," the agency "exercised against the grain of lines of domination," and the agency involved in processes of progressive social transformation.[15] The degree of voluntariness remains relevant: the fact that everyone has agency does not deprive us of the capacity for criticising conditions in which its exercise is particularly constrained. But like Michael Sandel (and Carole Pateman and Debra Satz and many others), I do not limit my social critique to the question of whether people freely chose.

I don't, however, find Sandel's corruption argument especially convincing. In his argument, goods have particular moral meanings, and their commodification is problematic when it involves treating them "according to a lower mode of valuation than is appropriate" to them.[16] There are many ways in which this could be applied to the body. We could say that human dignity is bound up in the way our bodies are treated; we could say the body is the temple of the Holy Spirit; we could say our identity as humans is bound up with our sexuality; we could say our identity as women is bound up with our capacity for reproduction. But just listing these makes it clear how very contested any such "valuations" will be. People do not agree on the moral meaning of the body, sex, reproduction, kidneys, blood, semen, or genes. So far as the body, moreover, is concerned, the fact that we uncontroversially send our bodies to market every time we agree to work for someone else makes it harder to locate a moral meaning in "the body" that could differentiate between problematic markets in intimate bodily services and unproblematic markets in anything else.

We All Have Bodies

The arguments I develop in this book rely partly on there not being such a stark divide. I argue, that is, that markets in sex or reproduction occupy the outer edges of a continuum that is, in some way, a feature of all labour markets. All paid employment subjects the body to external regulation and control. While the regulation is more extensive and intrusive in activities to which the body is central (sex work and surrogacy, but also, as Martha Nussbaum reminds us, professional football and ballet dancing[17]), the vulnerability associated with even a temporary loss of our authority over our bodies and selves remains—and should be more widely acknowledged—in activities to which the body is more incidental. It is not that selling sex or one's capacity to bear a child is so entirely distinct from any other kind of paid employment. Indeed, one of the lessons we can take from the analysis of the trade in intimate bodily services is the need to focus more closely on the embodied experience of all paid labour.[18] In recognising that many of the differences are differences of degree, we become more aware that anyone agreeing to work for another—in whatever sphere of employment—makes herself vulnerable to a loss of personal autonomy, and that she experiences this vulnerability through her body. In some areas of employment, the bodily experience is so negligible we barely notice it. In others it poses significant issues regarding health and safety at work. In others still, the regulation of the body and management of the emotions reaches what we should consider unacceptable levels. That there is a continuum does not mean we have no basis for criticising what is positioned on the outer edge.

But I also want to make a stronger argument that revolves around the fact that we all have bodies, and what I see as the implications of this otherwise banal fact for equality. Bodies function in my argument as that which reminds us of our shared vulnerability, that which alerts us to the common experience of living as embodied beings in the same world. Our ability to think of others as our equals is, in my view, very much bound up in our capacity to see those others as like us in at least some respect. One crucial way in which we are alike is that we all have bodies. The point, then, at which some people's bodies become the means to patch up the bodies of others—most dramatically, in the use of one person's body parts to save or enhance the body of another—is going to be deeply threatening to equality, and it is this, more than anything, that makes sense of the distinctions commonly made between donation (good) and sale (bad). There is a difference between the ways we might relate to the other in a context of donation—think of the stranger donating blood marrow or a kidney, but also the relative offering to bear a child, or even the friend offering to help us out with some sexual malfunction—and the ways we might relate to the other in the context of a sale. Donation encourages us to think more explicitly about our equality: to think about whether we would have been equally willing to provide the kidney, the pregnancy, or the sex, had we been in a position to offer this; to hope that had things been different, we would have been equally generous. A market in these things relieves the purchasers of the obligation to think themselves into the sellers' shoes. It occludes the equality that is otherwise expressed in the fact that we all have bodies.

All having bodies also functions in what may seem a more standard sense, highlighting the inequality that is an inescapable component in markets that depend centrally on the body. The argument I make here is not, however, just a version of Sandel's fairness objection; I am not claiming that no decision to trade in the body can be understood as voluntary because of the background inequalities. Inequality is a feature of many markets: we sell because we don't have enough; others buy because they have more. Yet a social division of labour would remain even in an imagined world of social, economic, and gender equality, because some, at least, of the social division of labour reflects differences in skills and preferences that lead you to specialise in one activity and me to specialise in another. We can tell a plausible tale about many specialisations that need not depend on the fact that you are rich and I am poor. But given that all of us have body parts, that most women of childbearing age can do pregnancy, and that most of us can do sex, what—other than the inequality—explains why some become positioned as buyers and others as sellers? This is a division of labour that is intrinsically linked to material inequality, not just (as with many other markets) contingently so. We could, at a stretch, say that those with two healthy kidneys have the "skill" to sell one, while those with malfunctioning organs lack the ability, but we could not plausibly claim that some people "prefer" to live with one kidney while others prefer to have two. When one person sells and another buys, inequality is the reason. The argument is somewhat more strained as regards surrogacy, for it is not entirely implausible to say that some women enjoy being pregnant while others either cannot or prefer not to be so, but as the global trade in surrogacy develops increasingly industrial conditions, most notably in India's surrogacy hostels, relying on "preferences" to explain the division of labour looks pretty unconvincing. As for prostitution, it is reassuring fantasy to imagine that sex workers have an unusual taste for sex with unknown and unchosen partners; they may indeed choose the job over others less well paid, but we cannot plausibly say they choose it because of their preferences and skills.

Property: "Good" and "Bad"

Reading the literature today, on the body as property, and the sale of bodily services and parts, I sense a hardening of resistance to notions of the body as special and greater accommodation with both literal and metaphorical commodification, including among those who would describe themselves as radical and/or feminist. Straws in the wind include the "new commodification" theorists, who argue that putting a price on things previously deemed untradable can shift power in the direction of the socially and politically marginal,[19] and a growing body of work that represents claims to the ownership of one's body or person as the means through which the average citizen can challenge the power of biotechnology companies.[20] Commenting on trends in commodification theory in her afterword to a recent collection on *Rethinking Commodification*, Carol M. Rose observes that "some commodification theorists are at least somewhat more comfortable with markets, and more intrigued with the market's possibilities for novelty, liberty, and self-fashioning—not to speak of money."[21] In some of these arguments, commodification itself is presented as a source of power; in others, it is the power of property that is defended, often precisely as a way of preventing commodification.

In this latter argument, seeing the body as special, or treating claims to body ownership as a travesty of our human dignity, deprives people of important protections against the market. In both English and North American jurisprudence, it has become a guiding principle that no one owns the body; that heirs cannot therefore claim property in dead bodies or body parts; that coroners have the authority to insist on burial or, in cases of postmortem, postpone it; and that people seeking to claim property rights in their own bodies are crossing an unacceptable line. Property rights in body parts or tissues have been recognised when someone subsequently exercises labour on it—when a technician treats and preserves part of a corpse, for example, for use as a medical specimen,[22] or a researcher for a large company uses it in research—but for the poor source of that body part, there is no recompense.[23] Many today see this refusal to acknowledge property rights in our bodies as leaving us with too little protection against medical malpractice or the rapacious activities of private companies. From this perspective, we need *more* property in the body, not less.

That property protects is one of the key claims commonly made on its behalf, and there is a long tradition of radical thinking that sees the assertion of property rights in one's self and one's body as the central challenge to slavery and a crucial part of establishing women as the equals of men. Slaves were not regarded as owning their own bodies: they did not have the right to refuse the sometimes impossible demands made upon them, they did not have the right to refuse intimate access to their bodies, and they had no legal recourse if their bodies were damaged or destroyed. Being able to assert ownership of one's body therefore disrupted the very foundations of slave society. In nineteenth- and much of twentieth-century Europe and America, nonslave but married women were also regarded as having no right to refuse their husbands access to their bodies (marital rape was not a crime), and for much of that period, married women were not regarded as capable of holding property in their own name. Being able to assert the right to own property, and, again, the ownership of one's body, proved crucial moments in women's mobilisation for equality.[24] Property has a radical as well as conservative history. My claim, nonetheless, is that framing bodily rights as property rights is not the way forward.

My minimal claim is that we do not need to assert property in the body in order to express what we mainly care about when we say "it's my body," which is bodily integrity. We have the right to stop other people doing things to or with our bodies. This is the basis for laws against rape and assault; for the right to refuse well-intentioned and life-saving medical treatment that nonetheless offends our religious beliefs; and for the belief that corporal punishment is a worse intrusion on human dignity than long-term imprisonment, even when the years spent in prison can be far more destructive and debilitating.[25] Framing threats to bodily integrity as if these are acts of trespass on private property is not, however, helpful. As J. W. Harris puts it, "the bodily-use freedom principle has whatever normative force it has without benefit of self-ownership notions. Property rhetoric in this context is unnecessary, usually harmless, but always potentially proves too much."[26] The language we adopt has consequences, and, as Lisa Ikemoto puts it, replacing "bodily integrity, decisional autonomy and equality" with "free market individualism and ownership"[27] affects the kind of society we create.

In what follows, I pursue my two questions—what's wrong with claiming ownership in the body? what's wrong with making bodies available for trade?—through case studies designed to highlight the risks of body property even where there are no obvious commercial implications, and the risks of body property when explicitly associated with markets in bodily services or parts. In chapter one, I expand on the difficulties in claiming the body as special and address some of the arguments for and against claiming it as property, before laying out the general grounds of my critique. In chapter two, I focus on rape, where the application of a property discourse is almost entirely metaphorical, with no direct implication as regards commodification.

I deal in this chapter almost exclusively with heterosexual rape, and with the rape of women's bodies, not those of girls or boys, for it is as regards the rape of adult women that the pull of property models has been most evident. In chapter three, I address markets in bodily services, focusing on commercial surrogacy rather than prostitution. Although prostitution would be the more obvious example, I want to tease out what it is about marketisation, as distinct from the activity, that can be regarded as problematic. Surrogacy is the more useful example here, because of the widespread distinction made between gift or altruistic surrogacy (usually deemed good) and commercial surrogacy (often deemed bad). In chapter four, I move on to markets in body tissues and parts, focusing on the most contentious trade—in live kidneys—and arguing that this relies on and undermines our status as equals. I also return in this chapter to those claims about property as protection, restating and developing my reservations about those who favour *more* body property as a means to resist excessive marketisation. In chapter five I turn to broad policy implications and argue that the individualism inherent in property claims makes it particularly difficult to engage with macrolevel concerns. Framing bodily rights as property rights constrains social policy in an overly individualist direction. Throughout the book, the fact that we all have bodies appears as a recurrent theme: it is in this, if anything, that the "specialness" of the body lies.

Markets change things, and so, I argue, does adopting a property discourse. We live in an era when developments in medical and reproductive technology present us with many troubling dilemmas about the extent to which the bodies of some can be employed to sort out problems with the bodies of others. Some of these may be temporary. It may be, for example, that further developments in medical science will make the search for transplant organs unnecessary, and that we will be able to make replacement organs as we currently make prosthetic limbs. But whatever the possible marvels of future science, we can be sure of one thing: that the number and range of these dilemmas will continue to grow. As we move forward on this difficult terrain, I believe we should stop and think, first, about whether we really wish to regard our bodies as property, and second, whether sending bodies to market is compatible with human equality.

CHAPTER ONE

What's So Special about the Body?

NO ONE THINKS IT A GOOD IDEA to treat people as if they were objects. We do not defend this even when we distrust notions of personal autonomy, or tolerate blatantly hierarchical relationships, for on any understanding of what it is to be human, people are not things. We talk of objects as inanimate or immoveable, and the power we most commonly attribute to them is that of being able to block activity. We may, of course, love our things. As Henry James warns in *The Spoils of Poynton*, we may come to feel more attached to the objects with which we surround ourselves than the people among whom we live. But objects remain objects, to be used, looked at, rearranged, traded, and perhaps ultimately thrown away.

Complaints about being treated as a thing have featured extensively in feminist writings, particularly as regards prostitution, pornography, and marriage, and in the analysis of advertising, the beauty industry, and film. The most persistent complaint is that women are treated as objects for someone else's (man's) satisfaction, or that women are "stabilised as objects," to adopt Simone de Beauvoir's evocative phrase.[1] There is often an associated argument to the effect that women then come to see themselves in the same light, that they accept the designation as object and participate in thinking of themselves in this way. In this argument, it is not just being treated as an object, passed on like a commodity, or regarded as someone's property that is the problem. It is that this can encourage you to think of yourself in a thing-like way.

Being an object, a commodity, and an item of property are not the same thing, and there will be some teasing apart of these different notions in the course of this book. There is a close enough connection, however, to alert us to an immediate puzzle. While no one wants to be regarded as an object, many like to think of themselves as "self-owners," like to see themselves, that is, as in a relationship of ownership to their bodies and selves. For the devotee of self-ownership, the rights we enjoy over our bodies closely parallel the rights the archetypical owner of property has over things. The right to bodily integrity, for example, can be refigured as the right to determine who has access to the body, in ways that mimic the rights a landowner has to exclude trespassers from his property. The freedom to sell one's labour (or, to use Karl Marx's more precise terminology, one's labour-power) can be treated as a version of the freedom any property owner might claim to decide for herself when and to whom to sell. For a small but growing minority, the actual body can also be regarded as an object available for trade: either the entire body, mortgaged off in anticipation of one's future demise, or those bits of the body (spare eggs, spare kidneys) we can currently manage without. In one representative comment, "because you own yourself and your labour, you must have the right to use your body and labour in any way you see fit consistent with the rights of others. So, if you want to sell your sexual services, you have a right to do so. If you want to sell your organs, you should be free to do so. If you want to take recreational drugs, it's your mind and body to do with as you see fit."[2] In this discourse, claiming property rights in the self is not represented as capitulation to a thing-like status. To the contrary, it is presented as protection: I am a free agent—hence the very opposite of a thing—to the extent to which I can claim ownership over myself.

We might dismiss this as a linguistic tic of right-wing philosophers, those so enraptured by the institutions of private property that they can only express their dreams of freedom and autonomy in its terms. There is, to my mind, something to this. But from John Locke onwards, claims to self-ownership have played their part in the elaboration of radical as well as conservative traditions; indeed, the quote above sums up a self-described *left* position, not one associated with the right.[3] This is not an issue that pits egalitarians against free-market libertarians, or those concerned to establish humane terms of social coexistence against tough-minded seekers after profit. In one feminist defence of the language, Rosalind Petchesky notes the importance attached to self-propriety in eighteenth- and nineteenth-century slave writings, and the significance of those moments when the "objects of property" asserted themselves as the subjects of property too.[4] If we think of self-ownership—in Ngaire Naffine's words—as "an assertion of self-possession and self-control, of a fundamental right to exclude others from one's very being,"[5] we can readily understand its appeal to the enslaved, subordinated, or oppressed. The capacity to resist intrusions on one's body (including through torture, rape, and forced marriage) is now enshrined as a central principle in conventions of human rights. This capacity can be, and sometimes is, formulated in ownership terms.

Does this matter? Any time we employ the possessive adjective, we are engaging casually with ownership language, but this is not to say we really think of our bodies or selves as property. The teenager who employs the rhetoric of ownership to defend her body piercing projects—"it's my body and I'll do what I like with it!"—does not mean she owns her body in the sense of having the right to cut it into portions and sell it to the highest bidder. The woman who says "it's my body" when asserting her right to determine for herself whether to have an abortion does not necessarily mean (though she may also think this) that she has the right to sell her sexual services as a prostitute or her reproductive services as a surrogate mother. We sometimes use the language without at all intending a property claim, or might genuinely mean to claim ownership, but without intending particularly extensive rights over use. J. W. Harris describes a musical jingle aimed at young children that tells them to "remember your body is your own private property, your body's nobody's body but your own."[6] Clearly, this is not intended to convey to children that they have the absolute right to do as they wish with their "property." The object is to warn them against inappropriate touching, and no one is suggesting they should feel free to decide for themselves which sexual favours to accord to which adult. Private property is invoked here to express the right to keep others off, not the right to invite them in.

In examples like this, we may think the choice of ownership language unhelpful, even incoherent, but might also consider this a somewhat pedantic point. Does it really matter if people employ the language of possessions to assert their rights to bodily integrity, or model their freedom on principles of private property? The visiting Martian who failed to appreciate the importance of property relations in our societies might regard this as a puzzling way to articulate notions of rights or autonomy or freedom. But given that property *does* play such a powerful role, should the widespread use of its language trouble us?

There is a long tradition of thinking that these ways of conceptualising the body and self *do* matter, some of it derived from Kantian prohibitions on treating others as mere means to ends, some from Marxist critiques of wage labour and the commodity relation, and some, more recently, from feminism. Kant was explicit about the prohibition on self-ownership: "Man cannot dispose over himself because he is not a thing; he is not his own property; to say that he is would be self-contradictory; for in so far as he is a person he is a Subject in which the ownership of things can be vested, and if he were his own property, he would be a thing over which he could have ownership."[7] Marxist critiques more commonly stress fetishism and alienation. It is not so much that owning oneself is a logical contradiction, but that thinking of oneself in this way expresses the dominance of capitalist relations, which having turned every conceivable object for human use into a tradable commodity now works to transform the very way we relate to ourselves. Writing in the 1920s, Georg Lukács saw the representation of people as owners of themselves as a final stage in self-alienation, the point where the commodity relation "stamps its imprint upon the whole consciousness of man: his qualities and abilities are no longer an organic part of his personality, they are things which he can 'own' or 'dispose of' like the various objects of the external world."[8]

More recently, Carole Pateman has drawn on Marx's analysis of wage labour to identify the "fiction" of property in the person, the way this conceals the subordination present in all labour contracts, but most starkly so when these directly engage the body.[9] Talk of "owning" one's body, body parts, or bodily capacities invokes what she terms the "masculine conception of the individual as owner, and the conception of freedom as the capacity to do what you will with your own."[10] Jennifer Nedelsky argues that thinking in terms of property encourages us to think of rights as held against others, and autonomy as achieved by building walls, and suggests that repeated use of property language can make the actual commodification of bodies more likely.[11] As applied specifically to women, she sees the language of property as strengthening what is already a tendency for women to regard their bodies as objects to be adjusted, slimmed down, and variously improved, in ways that encourage their self-alienation. Margaret Radin argues that "systematically conceiving of personal attributes as fungible objects is threatening to personhood because it detaches from the person that which is integral to the person." Like Nedelsky, she warns that "such a conception makes actual loss of the attribute easier to countenance."[12]

Objectification, Commodification, and Self-Ownership

I start with some preliminary definitions. I take objectification to mean treating a person, or aspect of a person, as if it were a thing. To employ more Kantian terminology, it involves treating human beings who are ends-in-themselves as if they were mere means. In slavery, sex trafficking, and wife selling, the person becomes literally an object, though even this remains a matter of degree, for people are mostly too recalcitrant to be consistently treated as things. Outside those extremes, the objectification is pretty much always metaphorical. Martha Nussbaum has suggested seven notions involved in treating a person as a thing: instrumentality (treating someone as a tool for your own purposes); the denial of autonomy (treating someone as lacking autonomy and self-determination); inertness (treating someone as lacking agency or even activity); fungibility (treating a person as interchangeable with other people or things); violability (treating someone as lacking boundary integrity, such that it becomes legitimate to break up or into); ownership (treating someone as a possession, as something that can be bought or sold); and the denial of subjectivity (treating someone as something whose experience and feelings need not be taken into account).[13]

Nussbaum's list broadly captures what we object to when we accuse someone of treating us like a thing, but we never find all the components together, and it is unlikely that any one of these could ever be experienced in full. I stress this because people sometimes try to resist accusations of objectification by pointing to some way in which the humanity of the person is still recognised even when elements of objectification are in play. It is hard, however, to conceive of human beings as *totally* interchangeable, *totally* inert, or *totally* lacking in autonomy. If we take objectification too literally and interpret it in too strict a way, we will too easily comfort ourselves with the belief that no one is ever objectified. The slave owner who notices that a slave has a fine singing voice, the client who is intimidated by the prostitute he has hired or, alternatively, who always asks for the same woman, are all recognising the existence of separate human beings who exist for themselves and not just as objects to serve the needs of others. Does this means there is no objectification going on? Beauty contests typically include interviews with contestants in which they are allowed to demonstrate that they are more than just a body, but are also interested in music or dancing or world peace. Does this mean there is no objectification going on? When we are dealing with people and their bodies, it is difficult not to notice, in some way, that we are dealing with people, not things. It is only in rare conditions—most notably war and even then not always—that people manage consistently to sustain an attitude of total dehumanisation. If we set the bar too low, such that the slightest recognition of another's humanity is evidence that they are not being treated as objects, we end up accommodating too much.

I follow Margaret Radin in employing the term *commodification* to mean both the literal buying and selling of goods and services and a discourse of commodification that "conceives of human attributes (properties of persons) as fungible owned objects (the property of persons)."[14] Radin takes the notion of fungibility from the definition of commodity employed in the US Uniform Commercial Code, where it is understood as the capacity to substitute one unit for another without any change in the value. The simplest illustration would be bank notes, which can be lent out and returned without anyone much caring whether the same note comes back, so long as it has the same denomination. Again, it would be a mistake to interpret this idea of fungibility too narrowly. Books can be commodities, and their substitutability lies in the fact that we are willing to exchange x units of books for y units of something else, or two blockbusters for one textbook, without feeling we have been shortchanged. But except in those apocryphal stories of people buying books by the metre in order to furnish their walls, we do not think just any book would do. The fact that we can conceive of swopping something does not mean it has no distinct or cherished characteristics of its own. By extension, it would not be an adequate response to accusations of commodification to note, in relation, say, to prostitution or commercial surrogacy, that clients often have strong preferences for particular types of women or strong attachments to particular individuals. Nor would it be an adequate response to criticisms of markets in body parts to claim that both buyer and seller exhibit some minimal awareness of the other's welfare needs.

Despite obvious overlaps, commodification is not the same as objectification. Something can be an object without being a commodity (the book is not a commodity when it is borrowed from a library); and people can be treated in an object-like fashion (as when women are ranked on the basis of their body shape or the clothes they wear) without being either available for sale or conceived of as anyone's property. We mostly talk of commodification and objectification when we think the language of commodity or object is being inappropriately applied; indeed, Stephen Wilkinson regards this as built into the meanings. "Just as it's not possible to objectify something which really is an object, it's not possible to commodify something which is really a commodity."[15] Both terms, in other words, carry a normative charge. This is why some say we should abandon the language altogether, for we do not describe processes we approve of as either objectification or commodification, and it might then be said we short-circuit the requirement for argument simply by our choice of term. I take this as a useful reminder that we need the argument as well. The point I would stress is that because commodification is a process rather than an endpoint, it too is unlikely ever to be complete. Noting the incompleteness is not an adequate answer to the charge.

Self-ownership eludes tight definition, and if the implied analogy is with owning something like a book or car, seems to fall apart as soon as you look at it.[16] If it refers to some inner self that owns the bits and pieces that make up the body and its capacities, it invokes an implausible mind/body distinction and begs the question of what is left of the self once these other bits and pieces are taken away. If it refers instead to a reflexive self that owns itself, why even talk of ownership? The relationship to commodification is ambiguous, for while it looks as if self-ownership is the precondition for commodification (how do body parts or bodily services get into a market unless the person whose body it is has ownership rights?), it is also—as noted in the introduction—represented as blocking commodification. This is what Peter Halewood describes as the "curious duality of meaning" in self-ownership,[17] the ways in which it asserts our control rights over ourselves, while simultaneously making it easier for us to relinquish them.

Feminism and the Body

My views on what it means to think of the body as property, and whether we can justify treating it as different from other "things," have been shaped by feminist theory, which has a long history of challenging objectification and mind/body dualism, and an almost equally lengthy engagement with the issue of prostitution. This has not, in the event, proved entirely helpful, for feminism points in almost opposite directions on these issues. Much of the existing trade in bodily services or parts centres on women's bodies (exclusively so as regards surrogacy and the market in human eggs, and predominantly so as regards prostitution), and some of the most powerful critics of both the metaphors of property and practices of commodification have been inspired by feminist concerns.[18] But feminist themes have also been prominent within "new commodification" theory, for the exclusion of certain activities from the market can be read as denying women fair payment for their work and confirming deeply conservative notions of them as tainted by too close an engagement with money and markets.[19] Katherine Silbaugh argues that "at a practical level, women should at least be wary of anti-commodification arguments, because these arguments arise when women receive money for something, not when women are paying money for something."[20] Many warn against representing women's identities as peculiarly bound up in their sexual or reproductive capacities, noting that this feeds into stereotypical images of women as saintly mothers. Claims about the specialness of women's relationship to their bodies are regarded as far too essentialising to count as justifications for treating the body as different.[21] While making the body special is, on some accounts, precisely what feminism does, this can also be read as sustaining images of men as defined through mind and women through hormones and bodies.

There has been particularly marked disagreement over prostitution and commercial surrogacy, where treating the body as special is seen as getting in the way of fair payment and equal protection for those who work in the sex trade or as surrogate mothers. Feminists disagree profoundly over the nature and significance of prostitution.[22] Some regard it as the quintessential expression of patriarchal power, legitimating not only the violence and abuse of prostitution itself but also the more generalised sexual abuse that permeates our societies. Others stress the continuities between sex work—their preferred term[23]—and other forms of body work, and argue that the stigma attached to prostitution makes it harder for sex workers to conduct their trade openly, organise trade unions, or seek the protection of the police against violence and abuse. The sale of intimate bodily services, it is said, is not so qualitatively distinct from the sale of other intimate services (Martha Nussbaum cites the philosophy professor, who takes money for her intimate search for understanding of the world and herself[24]), or so different from the ways in which all of us must use our bodies to make a living. Similar points have been made about commercial surrogacy. Carmel Shalev, later one of the architects of Israel's surrogacy laws, represents payment for surrogacy as a potentially revolutionary "wage for reproductive services" that draws attention to how much hard work is involved in pregnancy and childbirth.[25]

Feminism is not a unitary politics, and disagreement on such issues is not especially surprising. More important is the deeper analytical tension that underpins much of the disagreement, because while feminism provides compelling arguments against the mind/body dualism that informs many versions of body ownership, it also—by virtue of much the same arguments—deprives us of easy recourse to "the body" as dividing line. From most feminist perspectives, the body matters. Simone de Beauvoir's *Second Sex* is saturated with women's bodies; indeed, in my own first reading, as a prefeminist schoolgirl, I was far more interested in what I could learn about menstruation, sex, and marriage than her thesis about woman as Other. And while the bodies through which we live our lives are endlessly deployed to mark gender hierarchies, with men and women alike suffering from the disciplining of their bodies to achieve masculinity or femininity, feminism does not, on the whole, seek freedom in bodily transcendence. We live our lives and experience our subjectivity through our bodies, but the solution is not to pretend the body away.[26] Feminists more commonly want to reclaim its significance, challenging those who privilege mind over body, or seek to efface the particularities of the body in the pursuit of more general abstractions. It is widely argued, for example, that it matters whether the abstract individual who is the object of so much conventional legal and political analysis is (bodily) female or male,[27] and feminists typically challenge dichotomies between mind and body, reason and emotion, often identifying a strong gender subtext in the way these have been opposed.[28]

In its emphasis on lived bodily experience, feminism therefore provides a basis for criticising the mind/body dualisms that often underpin endorsements of self-ownership or arguments for a market in body parts, dualisms that treat the body as no different in kind from any "other" material resource, or regard it "as a form of external housing for the immaterial mind."[29] But if it is part of the objection to property discourse that it obscures the inseparability of body from self, this very argument also deprives us of easy distinctions between activities that involve the body and those that do not. The very pervasiveness of the body, even in activities we might otherwise deem cerebral, makes it harder to draw a line.

Feminist insistence on the embodied self thus provides ammunition for both sides of the argument about markets in bodily services and parts. Ronald Dworkin once wrote of drawing "a prophylactic line" around the body that would ensure that none of the egalitarian arguments for the redistribution of social resources could be taken as affecting our rights to our own bodies: bodies, in other words, should be recognised as different.[30] I too see grounds for distinguishing between bodies and "other" social resources, and hope to make a sufficiently compelling case for this in the course of the book. But so far as work at least is concerned, that prophylactic line is hard to draw. Martha Nussbaum notes that "all of us, with the exception of the independently wealthy and the unemployed, take money for the use of our body."[31] We cannot plausibly claim that some activities are lodged in the body while others float freely as activities only of the mind, or, at least, cannot plausibly claim this if we also want to insist on the self as embodied. This is the important truth in the defence of sex work. We cannot do any kind of work without dragging the body along, and a prohibition on the sale of any services that involve the body would make no sense at all.

We might distinguish, as Carole Pateman does, between activities to which the body is incidental and those for which it is the whole point. Prostitution would then appear on one side of the line and working in an office on another. But that seems incomplete, because we are happy enough for people to make a living through many activities to which the body is the point: dancing, for example, or professional football. Reservations about the sale of bodily services also cannot be based on a prohibition on touch, for this would rule out as inappropriate the physiotherapist, while ruling in as entirely unproblematic the surrogate mother, whose body need never be touched by the commissioning couple. A more plausible candidate, perhaps, is some notion of depth: the idea that intrusions deep into our bodies are more troubling to our sense of our selves than those that merely touch the surface. This fits with the unease most people feel at the prospect of live kidney sales as compared with their relative insouciance on sales of human hair. But the depth notion, too, is unsatisfactory, with its suggestion of a core, essential, "deep" self, surrounded by a more contingent periphery. The sale of any service requires the deployment of deep internal organs (we cannot do anything without our heart and lungs). If we think, moreover, of which aspects of our bodies we regard as most closely bound up with our identities, we are more likely to specify faces (surface) than kidneys (deep inside). It is not so easy to point to what it is about the body that makes it special or provides the necessary touchstone for separating out legitimate from illegitimate trade.

What's Wrong with Property?

The other problem area is property, now made especially problematic by the tendency to tell "good" stories of property alongside the "bad." Property as the unconstrained power to do as one wishes with one's own is mostly repudiated in today's literature, and theorists distinguish variously between weak and strong property rights,[32] control rights and income rights,[33] property as self-mastery and property as despotic dominion.[34] Mostly, these distinctions serve to alert us to the kinder face of ownership. Locke is sometimes invoked as inspiration for a more troublingly privatised understanding of property and Hegel as inspiration for an agency based understanding, where property links us to others and enables us to express ourselves in the world.[35] It is widely noted that property is not a thing but a relationship between people; furthermore, that it is a *bundle* of relationships, a bundle of rights, powers, and claims, not all of which need be present at the same time. In this disaggregated understanding of property, usually attributed to the work of Hohfeld and Honoré,[36] we can make a property claim about our right to manage, use, or keep others out of our property, without thereby also claiming a right to the income from the property, or the right to destroy it, or the right to sell. Our claims, moreover, always link us to others, for we cannot legitimately claim a property right in something without putting others under a corresponding liability or obligation.

Instead of all the focus being on property as exclusive and exclusionary power, property rights have therefore come to be understood as fashioned through legal and social relationships that regulate your claims on me as well as my claims on you. We sometimes think of the history of property as proceeding in unilinear fashion from property rights circumscribed by obligations, more typical of the feudal period, to the brutal assertions of private property associated with capitalism. This movement is typified in the land clearances in the Scottish Highlands in the eighteenth and nineteenth centuries, when people whose families had lived on the land for centuries were simply evicted. But the pattern has been more complex than this, with movements towards greater as well as lesser social obligation. Although there have undoubtedly been moments in history when people have asserted despotic dominion, it is hard today to think of any arena where the ownership of something conveys unlimited rights to do as you wish with your own. Property is circumscribed in a whole variety of ways, including through employment legislation, planning regulations, and taxation. Property owners are not necessarily at liberty even to determine for themselves who inherits their property, but may be required (in French and Spanish law, for example) to make provision for particular members of their family.

We might conclude from this—some do—that the presumed dangers in applying the language of property to persons or bodies are vastly overstated. We might say—some do—that property serves the weak as much as the powerful, and that claiming property in the body is the most effective way to secure the rights of those more marginal. People point to cases like *Moore v. the Regents of the University of California* (1988), where a highly profitable cell line was established from the unusual components of a patient's blood cells, while the patient himself was left in ignorance of what was being done.[37] Moore was treated for hairy-cell leukaemia at the medical centre of UCLA in the late 1970s and was asked to return on various occasions for tests involving the extraction of body substances such as blood, skin, and bone marrow aspirate. Unknown to him, his doctor and associated researchers were establishing a cell line from these; the university applied for and was granted a patent; and the researchers negotiated a lucrative contract with a major biotechnology firm. When Moore challenged this, partly on the grounds that he continued to "own" his cells after their removal from his body, he lost the case. California's Supreme Court mostly ducked the issue of whether one could own one's body tissues, reaching its decision largely on the grounds that allowing such ownership would seriously impede scientific research, but, in effect, *his* right to property in the body was repudiated, while the others' rights to property were affirmed. One judge described Moore's claim as a request that the court "regard the human vessel—the single most venerated and protected subject in any civilized society—as equal with the basest commercial commodity."[38] Moore lost to the might of the biotechnology industry and the supposed necessities of scientific research. Adding insult to injury, he was also criticised for treating his body as a commodity. One might think—some do—that in a case like this, it would have been more just to recognise his cells as his.

Or to take a middle position, one might agree that property in the body is a dangerous notion, but distinguish this from more innocent ideas of property in the person. Donna Dickenson endorses property in the person while challenging property in the body and argues that recognising the first provides us with the necessary tools to resist the second.[39] "People own their actions; they do not own their bodies."[40] It was this, she argues, that John Locke had in mind when he wrote of every man having "a property in his own person." We can usefully talk of owning our labour, and what we produce with it can then, in Lockean fashion, be understood as ours, but since Dickenson adheres to a "bundle of rights" understanding of property, this need not imply anything like the unconstrained right to sell. The ova extracted from women's bodies for the purposes of stem cell research or in vitro fertilisation should indeed, in her argument, be understood as their property, though not because they are part of the women's bodies but because they are produced by women's reproductive labour. The appropriate property rights attached to them would not, moreover, include the right to turn them into commodities and sell them on the open market, though they might well include the right to determine their subsequent use. In the case of surrogate pregnancy, the reproductive labour would again confer property rights, but not "full-blooded property rights over the child." It would require, rather, that "we recognise a limited set of property and contract rights such as protections against contracting couples who default if the 'surrogate' bears a disabled child."[41] Dickenson is particularly exercised by what she sees as the failure to appreciate the labour women perform and the risks to which they expose themselves, and she makes compelling points about the way "the lady vanishes" in controversies about stem cell research that focus almost exclusively on the ethical status of the embryos created but barely address the risks to the women who produce the eggs.[42] Recognising women as having property in their person, hence (limited) property rights in what they produce with their labour, would, in Dickenson's view, help change this.

I am not convinced by these more optimistic moves. My first reservation is that even the restricted claim to property in the person introduces an analytic distinction between capacities and self. This can seduce us, as Carole Pateman puts it, into "the political fiction . . . that capacities can be treated as separable from the person."[43] No one, of course, really thinks this (I don't for a moment charge Dickenson with this view), but once we describe ourselves as owning our labour, we are well on the way to an understanding that makes it analogous to a thing. Consider something Martha Nussbaum argues in her analysis of prostitution, that "the prostitute still has her sexuality; she can use it on her own apart from the relationship with the client, just as the domestic servant may cook for her family and clean her own house."[44] Nussbaum is saying here that the capacities are attached to us and that making them available to others, on occasion and for money, cannot then take them away. In one reading of this, she is echoing Pateman's point about capacities not being treated as if they are separable from the person. But if we reframe this in the language of ownership, the analogy that springs more immediately to mind is the taxi driver, who "still has" his cab and "can use it on his own" outside his taxi-driving work. When we refer to capacities as even analytically separate from persons—as the language of property almost requires us to do—we are drawn into analogies with things. To my mind, this seriously obscures what is going on in any kind of body work.

In talking of owning our labour or capacities, we suggest that contracting out their use is similar in kind to contracting out the use of a car: why else employ the notion of property? Intentionally or not, we represent work as the leasing out of capacities that just happen to be attached to a person. We focus attention on the beginning and end of the process: on the beginning, when the deal is struck, and we decide whether the terms are fair; on the end, when the payment is made, and the body and its capacities are returned to our exclusive use. The fact that "we" are present throughout their deployment (or, as one of my students once put it, that we supply a chauffeur along with the car) is either ignored or treated as unimportant. Yet the real drama of most work situations begins after the contract has been signed, as employers seek to exert their authority over those whose services they have engaged, and employees have to accept, negotiate, or resist demands whose full content may only become apparent at that stage.[45] When labour is treated as property, this normalises what remains a power relation. The relation will be more benign in some contexts than others: we are not all at the mercy of employers cranking up the pace of work and expecting more this year than they expected the last. Yet a benign exercise of power remains an exercise of power, however normalised and obscured by a language of property and exchange.[46] When employees internalise that language, moreover, and come to think of their labour as if it were indeed a separate entity, they live their working lives in what is plausibly described as a state of alienation. As Margaret Radin puts it, "they dissociate their daily life from their own self-conception."[47]

We cannot readily avoid this, for failing a Rousseauian idyll of self-employed farmers, most of us have to work for others at some point in our lives. The problem is that representing our labour in property terms makes the vulnerability less apparent. The metaphors of property encourage fantasies of the person as separable from her capacities and the self as separable from her body. In obscuring, and thereby softening, the nature of the relationship, the language reduces our vigilance when new demands are put upon us, limits our capacity for resistance, and may help convince us that nothing more can be done. This is certainly not Dickenson's intention—her own concerns about alienation and subordination closely parallel my own—but even on a fluid and more generous understanding of property, I find it perverse to look to property in the person as protection.

My second reservation about the more optimistic property tale relates to questions of reciprocity. When we frame bodily rights as property rights, we transform something that potentially connects us into something that keeps us apart. Bodies alert us to reciprocity and what we have in common, because all bodies need nourishment, all bodies feel pain, and all bodies are potentially vulnerable. In *Inventing Human Rights*, Lynn Hunt argues that the capacity to think in terms of universal human rights was associated, at least for theorists of the European Enlightenment, with the recognition that we can all feel pain.[48] Human rights, she suggests, became thinkable through a new preoccupation with bodily integrity and the development of an empathetic selfhood that alerted people to the universality of pain.[49] We came to think of very different others as nonetheless akin to us in their capacity for physical and emotional suffering, and ideas about bodily integrity were, she argues, a crucial part of this. Contrasting the mostly unquestioned use of torture in sixteenth- and seventeenth-century Europe with the increasing condemnation of both torture and inhumane punishment from the 1760s onwards, Hunt argues that this developed out a growing empathy with even justly accused criminals and a new concern for the human body. "Bodies gained a more positive value as they became more separate, more self-possessed, and more individualized over the course of the eighteenth century, while violations of them increasingly aroused negative reactions."[50] "Torture ended because the traditional framework of pain and personhood fell apart, to be replaced, bit by bit, by a new framework, in which individuals owned their bodies, had rights to their separateness and to bodily inviolability, and recognized in other people the same passions, sentiments, and sympathies as in themselves."[51]

I part company with Hunt in her claim about the importance attached to bodily integrity depending on notions of self-possession or self-ownership, but think she rightly stresses the connection between the importance I attach to *my* bodily integrity and the recognition that this also matters to *you*. There is an almost unavoidable reciprocity in the emphasis on the body, for all living beings have bodies, and what I experience through mine cannot be so totally distinct from what you experience through yours. I say "almost," and indeed recognition of that reciprocity has been much resisted, including to our own day. Hunt herself documents the very belated extension of human rights to those marked by their inferior sex or race, and Judith Butler's work on which lives are "grievable" testifies to our continuing capacity to erect hierarchies of pain, in which the grief suffered by distant or threatening strangers matters far less— perhaps not at all—than the grief of those closer to home.[52] Joanna Bourke's account of the stories people told themselves, well into the twentieth century, of the lesser pain threshold of "lesser" humans, and the inability of animals to feel pain, further warns us against Panglossian optimism.[53] But the very physicality of the body, as well as the fact that we all have one, keeps these hierarchies fragile. When a common humanity is grounded in a shared capacity for rational thought—as is more normally taken to be the message of the Enlightenment—supposed variations in intelligence or rationality are all too readily employed to justify unequal treatment. It is harder to do this when a common humanity is grounded in shared vulnerability.

People sometimes present property as also something we share. We all own something, it is said, even though some patently own more than others; we therefore all have an interest in maintaining the security of property even if some patently have more to gain. Yet this is a tenuous connection, and sometimes downright dishonest. At this point in the twenty-first century, it is difficult to think of territory or property without thinking of its unequal distribution, and appealing to people to respect the rights of property rings hollow to those who have so much less of it. A language of property is—probably inherently, but certainly now contingently—less capable of generating reciprocity than a focus on the bodies we share. If so, this is a further flaw in the case for conceptualising body rights in property terms.

My third reservation, particularly addressing the positive uses of property to resist commodification and prevent appropriation, is that "bad" property drives out "good." Although legal scholars are now almost universally committed to the disaggregated understanding of property, it cannot be said that people in general understand property claims in this way. Indeed, even some of those who explicitly endorse social constructionist understandings of property still claim "a person's right to sell an entity as the core feature of ownership."[54] Using property against property is a risky business, for we do not control the social meanings attached to the terms we employ, and it is all too likely that a restricted endorsement of property rights will be read in a more expansive vein. We can tell good stories about property, as Rosalind Petchesky does when she reclaims a "maternal, caretaking concept of ownership,"[55] or Stephen Munzer, when he associates property with the principles of preference satisfaction, justice and equality, and desert, and argues that no one of the three takes precedence.[56] These notions of what property is, or could become, may be entirely defensible, but popular understandings of property claims are still mostly mired in the world of absolute dominion, and there is a certain wishful thinking in imagining that this can be changed.[57]

And not just popular understandings, for those developments in the legal understanding of property also went largely unnoticed in G. A. Cohen's long engagement with Robert Nozick over ideas of self-ownership.[58] The issue there revolved around the relationship between the rights of the individual and noncontractual obligations to a wider community, the key question being how states could be justified in calling on their citizens for money or services—in essence, taxing us—if we "own" our selves. In Cohen's definition, "to own oneself is to enjoy with respect to oneself all those rights which a slaveowner has over a complete chattel slave," and "the polemically crucial right of self-ownership is the right not to (be forced to) supply product or service to anyone."[59] People may, on this account, agree to redistributive taxation because they can see some benefits, and social contract theorists have commonly argued that free individuals will contract to give up significant aspects of their property rights so as to gain political and economic security. But if you believe, as Cohen did, that people also have *noncontractual* obligations to one another, duties to help those less fortunate that are not grounded in enlightened self-interest, then the principle of self-ownership is incompatible with principles of justice. With hindsight, the whole debate seems premised on what legal theorists now regard as an outmoded understanding of ownership as the absolute right to control.[60] That outmoded understanding—property rights as akin to the rights a slave owner has over a slave—is more alive and kicking than defenders of the "good" property story would like to believe.

J. W. Harris regards claims to property in the body as "unnecessary, usually harmless, but always potentially [proving] too much."[61] I think the benefits are few and the risks greater than this suggests, and that we would do better to keep bodily rights and property rights in their separate boxes and not muddle the relationship between the two. The reasons for this are only partly grounded in the fear that thinking of our relationship to our bodies and selves in property terms will assist and normalise their commodification. Even where there is no danger of this, the adoption of property models is problematic. I turn, in the next chapter, to illustrate this through the example of rape.

CHAPTER TWO

Property Models of Rape

CLAIMS ABOUT PROPERTY in the body are often intended only as metaphorical and, as I have noted, many legal systems do not recognise bodies as the kind of "thing" that can be owned. Historically, rape appears the exception to this, for rape was long understood as an explicitly property crime. Not that it was conceived as stealing something from a woman. It was regarded, rather, as the taking from a father or husband of the potentially valuable commodity of a woman of reproductive age, and the offence was often punished by the payment of compensation to the father or husband. The very etymology of the English term, linking it to snatching or dragging away, locates rape as a property crime involving live prey. It was used to cover the abduction, not just of women, but of animals, children, and slaves, hence Louise du Toit's observation that "the connotation of sexual violation or sexual usage was not dominant in this [earlier] understanding."[1] The "stolen" women would typically be turned to sexual use, but it was their abduction that was the real crime.

Sexual violation later became more central to the definition,[2] but it was still the male who was regarded as the injured party, and his property, not hers, that had been damaged. As Susan Brownmiller puts it, "rape entered the law through the back door . . . as a property crime of man against man."[3] Nowadays, we tend to focus on consent as what distinguishes rape from consensual sex (I note later some problems with this), but consent was often beside the point in earlier times, for even in the unlikely circumstances where a woman *had* consented to her abduction, stealing her from the man still remained a crime. In seduction, too, it was the man who could initially claim damages, and it was his lack of consent that mattered, not hers. Although the legal offence of seduction was recodified in the course of the nineteenth century as a personal injury to the woman—who was then allowed to sue in her own name—it started out very much as a damages claim by fathers deprived of the value of the services of their daughters. In that understanding, the woman's consent was irrelevant. Not only did courts not need to establish that the sexual violation was nonconsensual, they could agree a claim for damages even if the woman *had* consented.[4]

Writing in Canada in the 1970s, Lorenne Clark and Debra Lewis argued that the property-based conception of rape still permeated popular and legal understandings: that women were still regarded as forms of property, and that rape was still considered a crime primarily because it devalued sexual and reproductive capabilities held in trust for men. It was this, they argued, that explained the greater willingness of the police to prosecute and of courts to convict when the raped woman lived at home with parents or a husband. Where a woman could be viewed as belonging to some man, her rape could be taken seriously as an offence against his property. But for the independent woman living on her own, they argued, rape would only be taken seriously if it involved severe physical injury. With no outraged man in the background, and no medical evidence of violent assault, there was (at the time) little chance of securing a conviction. In their analysis of this, "independent women . . . are seen quite literally as having no right to complain: since they cannot own themselves, and since rape is an offence against the owner of sexual property, such women are not viewed as having a legitimate complaint if they are raped."[5]

The claim had, perhaps, some plausibility for the period described, though even then I would be more inclined to stress the perception of women living on their own as sexually available and "asking for it," but that argument about rape as a property crime is not the one I want to pursue here. By the beginning of the twenty-first century, after several decades of feminist campaigning around the policing and legal treatment of rape, I do not think we can plausibly claim that rape is treated either as a crime against men or as a crime against male property. Important vestiges of this remain, most obviously in the use of rape as a weapon of war, where the violation of the woman is intended, in part, as an attack on the men of her community. Outside war zones, there is also a telling tendency for men to experience the rape of "their" women as an attack on their own masculinity and as damaging their own reputation. Although this might suggest women as the property of men and rape as an offence against those property holders, it also has its roots in notions of men as the protectors of women and women as responsible for family or community honour, and anyway, is not how rape is treated in most legal jurisdictions today. In a less pointed way, however, than Clark and Lewis argued, notions of rape as "an offence against the owner of sexual property" do continue to shape legal and popular understandings, though with the owner now clearly cast as the woman. This lingering property discourse significantly misrepresents the nature and experience of rape, primarily—if oddly—by making it possible for the body to disappear.

One would expect bodies to be central to any discussion of rape. But abstraction from the body has been a feature of much legal and philosophical writings, and the literature on rape turns out to be no great exception. At its extreme, some argue that it would benefit women if rape were explicitly aligned with theft, in ways that ignored or minimised the physical and sexual component. This is, admittedly, a minority position, but it is not so dissimilar to a more representative view of rape as the illicit appropriation of a woman's sexuality. In both versions, the property connotations can make everything turn on establishing the presence or absence of consent, delivering what Nicola Lacey describes as "a peculiarly mentalist, incorporeal" understanding of the harm involved.[6]

In more plausible vein, rape is sometimes conceptualised as a violation of bodily integrity, with the body then central to the understanding of the experience. (This is, in general, how I understand it.) But here, too, there is often a slippage into the language of property, as when the violation of bodily integrity is understood as a violation of personal territory, and rape is treated as the illicit crossing of a boundary.[7] Framed as an attack on bodily integrity, the occurrence of rape draws us together in the recognition of shared vulnerabilities and concerns, for all of us have bodies and all are vulnerable to bodily attack. Framed, instead, as a violation of territory, the occurrence of rape takes us into a discourse of property and property holders that is now irrevocably associated with inequality. Perhaps this was not always the case: perhaps when John Locke formulated his triad of "life, liberty and property," he genuinely thought he was naming three things that all of us share. But scholars have amply demonstrated that property could not have had universal significance at the time of Locke's writing,[8] and by our own times, it has become impossible to introduce notions of territory or property without conjuring up inequality. Bodies alert us to reciprocity and what we have in common; property alerts us to inequality and what keeps us apart; the choice of language then has significant implications. I shall return to this theme again.

Modelling Rape Explicitly on Property

I have noted that a number of contemporary writers believe a stronger endorsement of either property in the person or property in the body would provide people with better protection of their personal rights. Similar arguments crop up as regards rape. These often start from the historical observation that rape was initially conceived as a crime against men and go on to maintain that the failure to recognise *women* as property holders is a central part of what has hampered their recognition as persons. The argument depends on the privileged status accorded to property in contemporary market societies, and the way it has come to signify respect. "Property," claims Alexandra Wald, "signifies entitlement, undisputed possession and inviolability," and it is the "*refusal* [my emphasis] to view woman as property owners [that] facilitates the theoretical construction of women as 'exchange objects' or 'commodities.'"[9] Or as Catharine MacKinnon (not, herself, an advocate of property models of rape) observes, men never treat women's sexuality "in law or in life, with the solicitude with which they treat property. To be property would be an improvement."[10]

I start here with a version of the property model that would be repudiated by both MacKinnon and Wald and has not been taken up in any significant way but is useful in clarifying some of the implications of the property claim. In an essay in 1992, Donald Dripps proposed that rape be treated not as a violation of bodily integrity but as the illegitimate expropriation of property. He argued that this could significantly improve the rate of conviction on rape charges.[11] As he observes, juries have been reluctant to convict where there is a possibility that a women might have consented. In many jurisdictions, this has meant victims[12] have to establish the rapist's use of force, usually through medical evidence of physical harm, in order to have much chance of winning the case. Establishing that they were put under severe pressure to submit has not normally been enough. One could take this as reflecting a general difficulty in cases where one person's word becomes the main evidence against another's, or, more critically, as reflecting the belief that a woman's "no" really means "yes." Dripps claims that something else is also going on. A great deal of sex, he argues, is normally and legitimately traded, and it is the prevalence of legitimate, if often unsavoury, sexual bargaining that makes it difficult to secure convictions.

In his example of what he terms a "complex relationship," Ellen puts up with Frank's lovemaking (which is otherwise unwelcome) because she likes his companionship, enjoys the benefits of his high income, fears he might seek satisfaction elsewhere, and knows that "if rebuffed, Frank will be in a predictable snit for days thereafter."[13] Juries will be all too aware of this kind of relationship (some jury members may be implicated in like bargains), and this will make them particularly sceptical of what they see as retrospective claims about coercion. In Dripps's proposed solution, we would explicitly recognise sex as a commodity, as something we give, bargain with, and sell, and evidence that a victim had engaged in some such bargaining behaviour (hinting at a likelihood of sex, for example, in return for an expensive meal) would not, therefore, undermine her case. If we recognised sex as a commodity, this would stop the moralising about sexual bargaining; if we recognised sex as a commodity, the only question would be whether the sex was expropriated by illegitimate means. The central issue in rape cases would then become whether the rapist took the sex (stole it) despite an explicitly stated "no," and all the endlessly disputed signs of a victim's willingness or provocative behaviour would become beside the point.

As practical policy, this is not especially helpful; establishing that you said "no" when this is only your word against another's is unlikely to be so much easier than establishing in more circumstantial ways that you did not consent. The framing argument about a "complex relationship" in which one person extracts unwanted sex in exchange for letting the other share his income and house is pretty offensive, conveying a disturbing tolerance of partners who regard the provision of sexual services as their due. As Robin West objects, "friends do not impose unwanted sex on each other."[14] But it is her further objection that resonates most closely with my concerns. She notes that the "theft analogy wildly misdescribes the experience of rape," and strikingly omits "the violence, and hence the injury, of the penetration itself."[15] When rape is described as an illicit expropriation of property, the very tameness of the analogy obscures the bodily experience. It is notable, in this respect, that when Dripps explains why he regards rape as a *property* crime, and does not favour subsuming it under a general prohibition on *assault*, he offers as evidence the most disembodied of all possible scenarios: an unconscious victim who is entirely unaware of the violation and experiences neither physical harm nor subsequent discomfort. His analysis of what is essentially wrong with rape (not assault, but robbery) is achieved by imagining the body away.

In this overt form, the property model of rape wins few friends. At a more restrained level, however, it continues to inform much thinking, and Alan Wertheimer is not far off the mark when he claims that "the distance between the (ugly) property model and the (attractive) autonomy model is not very great."[16] The now standard legal definition of rape is nonconsensual sex. This rightly emphasises that it is the lack of consent, not the presence of threatening strangers armed with knives or guns, that characterises rape. It can also, however, encourage us to see consent as the magical ingredient that transforms an experience of rape into an experience of sex, in much the same way as consent can transform your theft of my car into an entirely innocuous borrowing. In one much cited—and heavily criticized—comment, Richard Posner claims that "all that distinguishes [rape] from ordinary sexual intercourse is lack of consent."[17] This provides us with an understanding of nonconsensual sex as what David Archard terms "sex minus consent" with the sex then treated as the common factor across both sex and rape, the only difference between the two experiences being that you wanted it in one case and not in the other.[18] When rape is represented in this way, the actual bodily experience (the supposed common factor) is bracketed out, and everything focuses on what was happening in the mind. Did the woman *agree* to what was going on? Did man *understand* that she was unwilling? Was it reasonable to *interpret* her behaviour as consensual? This is, indeed, a "peculiarly mentalist, incorporeal" way of identifying whether a rape has occurred. The job of the courts becomes to establish the presence or absence of consent, and "whilst that lack of consent is indeed mapped onto a bodily experience . . . nothing in criminal law doctrine invites any expression of the corporeal dimension of this violation of choice."[19]

I doubt if many will warm to the explicit assimilation of rape to theft, but treating the sex in "ordinary" intercourse as a more or less interchangeable experience with the sex in rape has much the same consequence. In both cases, there is some thing we might variously describe as sex, sexual services, or sexuality that is freely given, or perhaps slightly reluctantly traded, in one instance, but taken in the other. The language pulls us towards a discourse of property and things, and the specificities of the body disappear.

Bracketing Out the Body

In the case of rape, a lingering discourse of property and illicit expropriation rarely carries the risk of commodification. There have been moments when people have suggested that rape be decriminalised and turned into a mere matter for financial compensation, but this usually elicits robust rebuttals. Michel Foucault, for example, ventured the idea in a 1977 symposium on psychiatry and repression when he suggested that rape might be treated as a civil, not criminal, offence. The suggestion was bitingly repudiated by Monique Plaza, who immediately identified a commercial undertone: "There is no reason to forbid *rape*. Rape is permitted; the raped woman will 'simply' go and ask for damages. In other words, she will go to be paid for a sexual act that a man has committed 'with' her without her consent."[20] Treating rape as a damage to property that should be compensated by financial payment represents it as a kind of fraudulent—because unpaid—prostitution; this is not an approach that is likely to win much support. So, in the case of rape, the analogies with property are not going to lead to the commodification of women's sexuality or sexual services. The problem is that certain ways of thinking about rape encourage us to bracket the body out.

In the philosophical literature, this occurs mostly through the style of argument. Alan Wertheimer, for example, also rejects the notion of rape as a subcategory of assault and distinguishes between the physical injury caused when a rape is effected through violence and the harm of the rape itself, which he locates in the psychological distress caused by the sexual violation.[21] Fair enough, one might say, and certainly a good deal better than those endlessly repeated court proceedings where a charge of rape is dismissed because it has been impossible to prove physical injury. But he makes his argument by hypothesising a considerate rapist who offers to use K-Y jelly, using this example to establish that the offence of rape does not depend on physical injury or pain. I really doubt his understanding here: I doubt whether even the most generous dose of lubricant can eliminate the pain of unwanted sex imposed in an atmosphere of fear. As with Dripps's example of the unconscious and entirely comfortable victim, the analysis of what is essentially wrong with rape is achieved by imagining the body away.

The other argument that surfaces with some frequency calls on us to imagine away the *sexed* body. Rape, it is said, is currently misconceived by its association with sex and sexuality and should be redefined in ways that take the taboos about sex out of the picture. This was a particularly prevalent view in the 1970s and '80s, when it was argued that the representation of rape as an especially heinous crime reflected outmoded notions of the sanctity of sex, and that it would be better to remove the sexual component and treat rape "just" as physical assault. In one representative comment, Michael Davis describes rape as a serious crime but "*not* a *very* serious crime. Rape should be treated as a variety of ordinary (simple or aggravated) battery because that is what rape is."[22] Battery—unlawful touching—is bad, but if we were offered a choice between unwanted sex or having a leg permanently crushed by a car, surely most of us would "choose" the rape? The schedule of punishments ought, he argues, to reflect this, and he anticipated that under his proposed redefinition of the crime, the "typical rapist" would serve a maximum prison term of six months. Just one month might be appropriate for the rapist who "merely threatens his victim with bodily harm if she does not do as he says."[23]

This is a pretty startling diminution of the harm of rape, yet in the cluster of arguments calling for its desexualisation, there are a number that are broadly progressive. Lorenne Clark and Debra Lewis also argued in favour of treating rape as physical assault (though they clearly had a more serious schedule of punishments in mind), because they saw this as making it clear that it was an attack on the person and not on property.[24] Davis himself appeals to the authority of Susan Brownmiller, concluding his article with a quote from *Against Our Will* to the effect that recognising sexual assault as an injury to a woman's bodily integrity—not, as at some earlier periods, to the man whose property is defiled—means we could "normalize the penalties for such an offense and bring them in line more realistically with the penalties for aggravated assault, the crime to which a sexual assault is more closely related."[25] In that 1977 panel on psychiatry and repression, Michel Foucault also broached the issue, addressing it in the context of his general critique of the regulation of sexuality. Although somewhat tentative about whether his opposition to the policing of sexuality should extend to include rape and sexual relations between adults and children, he suggested that there might be "no difference, in principle, between sticking one's finger into someone's face or one's penis into their sex," and that only the physical violence should be punished.[26] For Foucault, it seems, rape was "sex plus violence," and he feared that punishing both the violence *and* the sex would strengthen the hand of those who are always so keen to regulate sexuality. Archard's argument about the mistake of thinking of rape as "sex minus consent," as if the sex were a constant factor between rape and "ordinary" sex, is particularly apposite here.

In a later contribution, Harriet Baber makes a case for the desexualisation of rape that draws on explicitly feminist concerns.[27] She argues that representing rape as the supreme violation and humiliation encourages a perception of women as more defined by their sexuality than men, and more likely than men to experience the violation as deeply damaging to their sense of identity. It represents women, that is, as having a different kind of relationship to their bodies than men: women's bodies as special. Thinking of rape in this way, she argues, reinforces women's status as sex objects. More importantly, it obscures the greater damage done to women's welfare interests through their concentration in low-skilled routine employment, for the harm of rape, she argues, is considerably less than the systemic and mind-limiting harm of working as a cashier or assembly line worker. This part of the argument reverberates with a mind/body dualism that disparages the merely bodily and elevates that which promises to stretch the mind, as when Baber suggests that "rape *per se* merely violates the victim's sexual integrity. The work that most women do however violates their integrity as intellectual beings." Rape is "bad, indeed, very bad. But being a keyboard operator is worse."[28] Quite apart from the mind/body dualism, I am struck by the breathtaking patronage towards women in nonprofessional occupations.

Challenging images of women as having a special kind of relationship to their bodies, and seeking to reduce the sexual connotations of rape, are not crazy ideas. The last, in particular, resonates with widely shared feminist views about rape having nothing to do with a desire for sex and everything to do with violence and domination, and it is not inconceivable that reducing the sexual connotations could help reduce the inappropriate sense of shame and defilement many survivors describe. The common feature of these arguments, however, is that the bodily experience is sidestepped, expunged, or just poorly understood. This is one important consequence of applying property discourse to rape. It is not that women's bodies or body parts or sexual services are represented as detachable and tradable commodities, or that talking in this way makes it more likely that they will be traded. It is, rather, that the relationship of self to body is represented as an *external* relationship between two distinct entities, to the point where rape can no longer be recognised as embodied experience. The failure to grasp the pain and violence of rape, except when "aggravated" by a physical beating or knifing, is one indication of this, but so too are the attempts to identify what is essentially wrong with rape by imagining the body away. When we pattern the relationship to the body on ownership—as when we think of women as owning a sexual property in their bodies and regard rape as the violation of their property right—it becomes particularly difficult to bring the bodily experience into focus.

Boundaries and Boundary Crossing

The above focuses on property discourses that treat sexuality as something that can be "taken," but property also (and somewhat more plausibly) enters the discussion as a spatial language of boundaries, zones, and domains, with rape then represented as an illegitimate border crossing. Joan McGregor provides one example of this when she argues that "sex, sexuality, our bodies and control over them are central to who we are," and that "rape is such a serious violation because it transgresses this central zone for our identity."[29] In this account, there is no suggestion that the body or bodily experience is being discounted. To the contrary, the body is explicitly conceptualised as part of our domain and "the physical locus of the person."[30] My worry here is that the deployment of territorial language encourages us to equate bodily integrity with securing the borders. This denies sexuality as activity, constitutes others as intruders, and recommends *dis*connection as the route to autonomy and self-control.

There are a number of problems with this. Conceiving of rape as an illegitimate border crossing threatens to turn female sexuality into thing rather than activity, and can thereby contribute to symbolic objectification. As Sharon Marcus puts it, "the psychological corollary of this property metaphor characterizes female sexuality as inner space, rape as the invasion of the inner space, and antirape politics as a means to safeguard the inner space from contact with anything external to it. The entire female body comes to be symbolized by the vagina, itself conceived of as a delicate, perhaps inevitably damaged and pained inner space."[31]

Conceiving of rape as illegitimate border crossing also invokes a language of property and boundaries that constitutes others as intruders. Criticising "the deeply ingrained sense that individual autonomy is to be achieved by erecting a wall (of rights) between the individual and those around him,"[32] Jennifer Nedelsky argues for a conception of selfhood as enabled, not threatened, by our relationships with others. Property, she argues, does indeed provide the language of self-respect and independence for which it is so widely praised, but it also becomes "the central symbol" for an exclusionary and protective understanding of autonomy, "both literally and figuratively provid[ing] the necessary walls."[33] She proposes instead a relational understanding of autonomy where "what is essential to the development of autonomy is not protection against intrusion but constructive relationship,"[34] and insists that "our project should not be to try to shore up women's boundaries."[35] This last injunction is of particular significance when we consider the fear of others that is so often described as part of the traumatic aftermath of rape. If we conceptualise rape as a violation of territory, we may come to think of recovery as a reassertion of boundaries and rebuilding of walls; to revert to the burglary analogy, we may respond to the violation by installing better surveillance equipment, adding more locks, and refusing to admit any strangers. Maybe this works for some, but it hardly addresses what Nedelsky describes as the "shattering of self-in-connection,"[36] or what Susan Brison highlights as a crucial need to *re*connect with humanity.[37] It is not that the language of invasion is entirely inappropriate, but if we think of what it is that is so painful about rape, and why (contra Michael Davis) its effects can last so much longer than those that arise from being physically assaulted, I suspect it is something about the way rape forces your involuntary involvement. As violations of bodily territory, being raped and being knifed look very similar. But there is nothing about being knifed that makes you even an unwilling participant; it does not simulate something in which you normally play an active part; it does not force you, against your will, to be a part of what someone else is doing. The violation in rape is relational as much as territorial.

Both violation and territory are problematic terms: *violation* because it suggests an attack on something previously held sacred or pure (the inviolate); *territory* because it marks out property, and we cannot now conceptualise property without thinking of it as held in unequal amounts and potentially threatened by intruders. The language of bodily integrity has its problems too, seeming to imply an already constituted unity, and understating what has been described as the "leakiness" of bodies,[38] but it has the great advantage of naming something we all have and need. Relationship and reciprocity are already implicit in the notion of bodily integrity. In drawing attention to my own bodily vulnerability, I cannot consistently deny that you face the same concerns. If, by contrast, I describe my need for bodily integrity as if it were a concern with territorial integrity, this turns something that potentially links me to other living beings into something that keeps us apart.

Experience—In What Sense?

I have said that bodily experience is central to understanding the nature and harm of rape, and that property discourse makes this harder to grasp.[39] But what does it mean to make the bodily experience central: "experience" in what sense? One of the areas of disagreement in the philosophical literature has been over whether the wrong of rape is better understood in objective or experiential terms, and there are plausible arguments on both sides. An objectivist version—grounded perhaps in an understanding of personhood, or a claim about the centrality of bodily and sexual integrity to the sense of self—looks better able to deal with the different ways we relate to our sexuality.[40] There is something offensive in making the wrong of rape depend on how much it upsets the victim: in saying, for instance, that raping a prostitute is a lesser crime, because prostitutes have developed a greater capacity for separating themselves from their sexuality; or that raping a man is a lesser offence because men have learned to be more resilient; or that raping someone who has regarded sex as a pleasant pastime is a lesser crime than raping someone who is saving herself up for the love of her life. If the wrong of rape becomes a function of the victim's distress, this threatens to legitimate what is already a major element in the low conviction rate: the tendency to dismiss as less compelling the claims of those with a more varied sexual history. It also seems to require victims to ratchet up the intensity of their distress in ways that can make recovery more difficult to achieve.

Against this, an objectivist account threatens to tie us to potentially dubious claims about what constitutes personhood and attaches insufficient weight to historical and cultural variation. In David Archard's version, rape is "an indefensible harming of a legitimate interest in safeguarding what is central to our personhood,"[41] and this is so regardless of how central any specific individual actually considers sex to her sense of self. "Each of us is a sexed being such that our sexuality, our sexual nature, is central to our identity, to who each of us is."[42] This is not meant as an empirical claim—he goes on to say that "this does not mean that each of us is sexually active, or thinks often about sex, or is deeply interested in sex, or is continually moved by sexual desire"—but is grounded in a conception of human flourishing. As such, it provides a more defensible way of addressing the wrong done to sexually experienced rape victims, but is vulnerable to the objection that it overstates the centrality of the sexual in personal identity. Attempts to specify the central capacities for human flourishing are notoriously open to critique.

The other way of putting this is to say that the objectivity version lends itself to worries about cultural specificity. Where, we might ask, does this conception of human personhood come from, and how closely does it reflect the preoccupations and self-understandings of specific human societies?[43] I have stressed that the pain and humiliation of rape is a bodily experience, and I see the physical pain as pretty much independent of social conventions or beliefs. But the ways we inhabit our bodies are clearly mediated through our understanding of social and cultural norms. What we experience as humiliation and violation is no simple fact, to be given its due (or not) in the way a society polices and punishes rape, but is something we create, sustain, and could perhaps change, in the way we live our lives. Different discourses of rape can then mean not just different attitudes to bodily experience, but genuinely different experiences.

At this point we face the troubling thought that we could make rape a more or less distressing experience by the way we define and understand it. Is this the kernel of truth in those otherwise implausible assimilations of rape with assault or theft: that taboos about the body and sexuality can make matters worse rather than better for rape victims? When rape is represented as the worst thing, short of murder, that can happen to a woman, perhaps this becomes part of the trauma, doubling back on the experience of harm to make recovery even more difficult? Part of the harm of rape *is* that it is wrongly perceived as destroying one's worth. In some societies, a raped woman is regarded as defiled, becomes unmarriageable, brings dishonour on her family, and is forced to hide herself away. But even when such notions are explicitly repudiated—when the value of women is not generally considered a function of their virginity, and women are not primarily regarded as the custodians of family honour—the violation is still widely experienced as damaging self-worth. Raped women do not talk easily about their experience in any society, and neither do raped men. It is, indeed, one mark of the incongruity of treating rape as akin to either assault or theft that we commonly exchange tales of being attacked in the street or robbed of our property without any sense that we are revealing something private about ourselves or exposing a humiliation.[44] Even in times when sexual matters are discussed relatively freely, it is rare for either women or men (perhaps especially rare for men) to talk openly about an experience of rape.

Jean Hampton urges us to distinguish between diminishment ("the mere portrayal of someone as lower"), and degradation ("the actual lowering of a person's value").[45] She regards rape as deeply wounding—diminishing—in conveying the idea that women are just objects to be used by men, but she insists there is no way it can actually degrade us, for the equal value of each human being is independent of anything others may do or say. I take her point, but it is hard in practice to keep these apart. The fact that rape does not *actually* make women inferior or *actually* transform them into sex objects may carry little force in the face of a sustained assault on the sense of self-worth. We cannot deal with the assault simply by affirming Hampton's distinction. It seems important also to challenge particular understandings of sex or sexuality that may be contributing to that sense of degradation. The worry is that this brings me back to some of the positions I have been criticising, where we think we can change the meaning and experience of rape by redefining it away from the bodily experience or changing how we understand it.

Some would say, at this point, that we simply cannot do this, that rape *is* experienced as violation and degradation, and that no amount of redefinition can change this. This is broadly the line adopted by Wertheimer, who provides an experiential account of the harm of rape but counsels against the view that because it is experiential, it is therefore readily changed. He believes that rape and nonconsensual sexual relations "are special harms largely because they are experienced as special harms," but also that "the distress to women caused by sexual violation is deeply implanted in the human psyche."[46] His analysis is grounded in an evolutionary psychology that represents women as less likely to desire sex than men and, by extension, more likely to experience nonconsensual sex as distressing. Since he regards the aversion to nonconsensual sex as "at least partially hard-wired,"[47] the fact that it is based in experience does not make it more open to transformation. If the distress were caused by what he describes as culture or a particular set of beliefs, we might plausibly limit the distress by changing the culture or beliefs; he considers this the appropriate course of action, for example, for the distress experienced by some people on seeing a same-sex couple holding hands.[48] With the sense of violation associated with rape, however, this is not an option.

I have numerous problems with this account: the evolutionary psychology itself; the suggestion that an aversion to nonconsensual sex is a function of the desire for sex (so people who like sex don't so much mind being raped?); and the largely unargued contrast between the pliable distress associated with homophobia and resistant distress associated with sexual violation. My key objection, however, is that it only deals with the yes/no question of whether nonconsensual sex will continue to be experienced as a harm. The answer to this is surely *yes*: rape is and will continue to be experienced both as physical violence and as violation. But the precise nature of that violation shifts through history, so if this is meant as a claim about the timeless experience of rape, it is surely implausible. Joanna Bourke points to evidence that rape has "*increasingly* become a sexual attack," and argues that the distress of rape for working women in nineteenth-century Europe would have centred less on the attack on their sexuality and more on the damage to livelihood and respectability.[49] The "intense focus on the body as marker of identity and as a locus of truth is a profoundly modern conception,"[50] and the notion of rape as destroying one's sense of identity is, Bourke argues, very much a feature of the late twentieth century. The physical pain of rape may be cross-cultural and timeless, but the nature of the humiliation and degradation, and the way this is understood by victims, is likely to vary according to context.

Suggesting that rape can be made a more or less traumatic experience depending on the significance attached to virginity, respectability, or sexuality is troubling. It threatens to trivialize the experience and can give the impression that the victims are at least partially responsible for their own sense of harm. At its worst, it sounds like some of the arguments associated with Camille Paglia or Katie Roiphe: the idea that women should be tough enough to accept the risks of their own sexuality, or should stop treating an unpleasant or subsequently regretted sexual experience as if it were rape.[51] Even when rape is clearly recognised as rape, describing it as "a question of language, interpretation, and subjectivity"[52] introduces what may seem an inappropriate indeterminacy. When that claim is combined—as in Sharon Marcus's controversial formulation—with a description of the "rape scripts" that reinscribe women's helplessness, and a call for women to disrupt the "rape narratives" that enable the violence of rape, this lends itself to interpretation as a kind of victim blaming. At least one critic reads Marcus as holding feminist discourses that stress male power partly to blame for the high incidence of rape, because they contribute to women's failure to adopt a sufficiently combative response.[53]

I do not know if women could more successfully fight off rape attempts if narratives of masculine power and feminine helplessness did not make us liable to paralysis. I do not know if rape survivors could more effectively deal with the trauma if they were enabled to think of the experience as less threatening to their core identity. Susan Brison provides some compelling evidence to the contrary when she describes the very *physical* character of traumatic memory: the way "traumatic flashbacks immobilize the body";[54] the attempts by survivors to change the appearance or size of their body, usually so as to make it more invisible; or the dissociation from the body, the most extreme version being the creation of multiple selves. This clearly warns against any glib suggestion that women might recover easier and faster if they just stopped attaching so much significance to the rape, though Brison also stresses—indeed this is a central part of her argument—the importance of stories in the healing process, and the way survivors learn to reconnect with humanity through the telling and retelling of their experience. As regards rape, it seems we are continually torn between needing to persuade society, police, and law courts to take the offence more seriously and needing to reassure ourselves that rape is not the end of our world. The first usually involves documenting the occurrence of rape and its traumatic consequences. It can then be at odds with the second, for it may involve what Rachel Hall calls "the performative recurrence of horror"—"spectacular presentations of sexual violence statistics; apocalyptic narratives of rape as a fate worse than death; the fatalistic belief that violence inheres in sexual difference"[55]—that combine to make recovery more remote than before. I do not have easy answers to this, but I am at least certain that thinking of rape in property terms is no help at all.

Those who explicitly recommend a property model of rape are in a minority, and I do not claim this either as the dominant view or as likely to become so. I have sought to establish that the minority view is both unhelpful and harmful, that it "wildly misdescribes," as Robin West puts it, the experience of rape, and omits "the violence, and hence the injury, of the penetration itself."[56] But I have also argued that the bracketing of the body that is so marked a feature of explicit property models characterises more standard understandings as well. When rape is treated primarily as a mind crime—as "sex minus consent"— the body is also bracketed out; the body that links us to every other body disappears. We all of us have bodies—men as well as women—and all can experience pain and fear. When rape is represented in ways that minimise the significance of this, something that potentially alerts us to a shared vulnerability is reduced to a minority concern. The distancing and fragmentation is characteristic of property language, even when this is not explicitly applied.

CHAPTER THREE

Bodies for Rent?
The Case of Commercial Surrogacy

IN MY DISCUSSION OF RAPE, I was concerned with the way a language of property can misrepresent the harm of rape, making it harder, rather than easier, to recognise shared vulnerability. In many cases, the misrepresentation also understates the harm, but I have not tried to argue either that explicit property models are dominant or that recourse to them directly affects the way police forces treat rape victims or courts process charges of rape. Nor have I argued that a property model has direct consequences as regards the marketing of bodily services or body parts. One could think of rape as theft or as territorial violation without thereby committing oneself to the view that people should be encouraged to sell that which can be stolen, or feel free to charge for territorial violations. Here, I turn to the sale and purchase of intimate bodily services, where the connections are more direct. When a market develops in intimate bodily services, this suggests that the bodies with which they are performed have come to be regarded, in some sense, as property, and therefore available for trade.

This is not necessarily the *self* description, for while there is evidence that some sex workers find the language of owning their bodies empowering,[1] those involved in the sale of bodily services sometimes object strongly to descriptions of the transaction in property terms. Even if endorsing the looser formulation of "it's my body and I can do what I like with it" (not all will endorse even that), they do not normally describe their activities as the "renting" out of a body for commercial use. For many of those most closely engaged in the commercial transaction, it turns out to be important *not* to embrace notions of body property. This widespread discomfort with the language of property amongst those whose activities otherwise seem to embrace it strikes me as itself a significant indictment.

I return later to the complexities of identifying some activities as "intimate" bodily services, in contrast to others where the body is incidental or less intrusively engaged. For the moment, I simply adopt the conventional understanding, in which prostitution and commercial surrogacy appear as two leading examples of markets in intimate bodily services. These clearly differ in significant ways—and many will regard the linking of them as offensive[2]—but one cannot but notice that the first is overwhelmingly associated with the female body, and the second exclusively so. The sale of sexual services has been with us for millennia, is widely condemned by moral and spiritual leaders (some of whom later turn out to be clients), and is regulated in most countries by criminal sanctions, some of which bear more heavily on the prostitute and some on the client. The sale of reproductive services is of more recent origin and has been dramatically boosted by techniques of assisted reproduction that make it possible to separate out sex from reproduction and genetics from gestation. It, too, is often regulated by criminal sanctions, though the target of these is more commonly the agency running a surrogacy business than the surrogates themselves. It is legal, however, in a number of jurisdictions, including India, some parts of the United States, the Ukraine, Israel, Thailand, and

Georgia, and agencies based in these countries advertise their services worldwide.

What is mostly understood by surrogacy today is one of three types: a woman becomes pregnant through artificial insemination, having agreed to relinquish any child born from this to the genetic father and his partner; a woman has a fertilized egg implanted in her uterus, having agreed to relinquish the child to the commissioning parents who have provided the genetic material; a woman has a fertilized egg implanted in her uterus, created with donor ovum or donor sperm, having agreed to relinquish the child to the commissioning parents, only one of whom is also a genetic parent. Surrogacy websites sometimes normalise the practice by recounting the bible story of Abraham and Sarah, in which the childless Sarah offers her handmaiden Hagar to Abraham, so that she can "give" him a child. I imagine childless couples have been making similar surrogacy arrangements from time immemorial, though describing this as the action of "couples" no doubt overstates the sense in which it is jointly pursued. It was, however, the medicalisation of reproduction, first through refinements in artificial insemination, then with the development of in vitro fertilisation (IVF), that made it possible to employ a surrogate without having sex with her and without even requiring her eggs. What is now known as gestational surrogacy is by far the commonest form these days, and it is particularly with this development that the commercial markets have flourished.

In India, where the income gap between surrogates and commissioning parents is stark, commercial surrogacy has become "a survival strategy" in some poorer rural areas,[3] and websites advertise the service as a quick and easy way to achieve one's "own" child. Commissioning parents are told they may only need a week's visit for the initial IVF procedures, followed by two weeks at the end of the pregnancy to collect the baby or babies, and a significant proportion of them travel from outside India, from the United States, Southeast Asia, or Europe. In Israel, where pronatalist policies have encouraged the development of technologically assisted reproduction, surrogacy was legalised in 1996, though under carefully controlled conditions that prevent the use of donor sperm, require surrogate and commissioning parents to be of the same religion, and require all contracts to be approved by a government-appointed committee.[4] In the United States, some states ban surrogacy contracts or treat them as unenforceable, but the trend across the country as a whole is towards accepting commercial surrogacy and providing greater statutory protection for the commissioning parents. In particular, should a gestational surrogate change her mind at the end of the pregnancy, she has little chance of claiming the right to care for the child.[5] An estimated one thousand contract pregnancies are arranged each year, surrogates are paid in the region of $30,000, and the total cost to commissioning parents, including legal, agency, and medical fees, is two to three times this.[6]

With both prostitution and commercial surrogacy we encounter something that looks like the renting out of the body. The woman is paid for the use of her body (this could be for a matter of minutes with prostitution, but nine months for a successful pregnancy) in ways that seem to parallel the renting out of a house or car. This is clearly not the sale of a body, and definite limits are set as regards the length of time and the uses to which the body can be put, but clear limits are also set to time and usage in rental agreements involving houses and cars. It might then seem entirely appropriate to describe the activities as renting. This, certainly, is how many commentators talk of it. Referring in 1987 to the famous *Baby M* case, where the surrogate mother changed her mind during the pregnancy and sought to keep the child, historian Lawrence Stone managed the double act of defining both prostitution *and* surrogacy in this way. "Contracts," he argued, "should be fulfilled. This is rather a bizarre contract, I agree. You're renting out your body. But one expects a prostitute to fulfil a contract."[7] A recent study of the surrogacy industry in India reports the broker and matron of one surrogacy hostel using the rental metaphor to convince potential surrogates that the transaction is morally acceptable (that is, *not* prostitution): "To convince the women I often explain to them that it's like renting a house for a year. We want to rent your womb for a year, and Doctor Madam will get you money in return."[8]

Mostly, however, the association of surrogacy with the renting out of a womb or prostitution with the renting out of a vagina is regarded as overemotive and offensive. Renting suggests, among other things, that the person vanishes during the period of the transaction; this diminishes the woman and denies her agency. We do not make this uncomfortable parallel in other instances where people are selling bodily services. It would be unusual, for example, to suggest that the model in a life class is "renting out" her body, or that she becomes less of a person just because she is being paid (as she clearly is) for its use. It is striking, nonetheless, that the property discourse is so resolutely rejected by most of those engaged in prostitution or surrogacy, and especially strongly by those engaged in the latter. While advocates of self-ownership encourage us to think that it is *because* we own our bodies that we should be free to sell our sexual or reproductive services as we wish, this is not the standard narrative among those engaged in the sale. In interviews with surrogates in India, Amrita Pande more commonly heard narratives that played down the right to choose and represented the decision to become a surrogate as a bowing to economic necessity.[9] Rutvica Andrijasevic found a similar disavowal of agency among Eastern European women working in street prostitution in Italy, who also stressed that they were "forced into" the work and "had no choice." She sees this denial of agency as part of what enables the women to live with the work.[10]

I focus here on surrogacy rather than prostitution, because with surrogacy it is easier to separate out concerns about commodification from concerns about the activity itself. With prostitution, the two are almost impossibly entwined. Prostitution is not just sex plus payment (any more than rape is "sex minus consent"), for outside the world of prostitution, people do not normally engage in sex with multiple unknown and unchosen partners, on terms in which only one person expects to experience pleasure. The sale shapes and defines the activity, and when people criticise prostitution, it is not just the fact of payment they object to but what that payment does to the nature of the sexual encounter. It would make no sense to say there is nothing wrong with prostituting yourself so long as you don't get paid. If we are to separate out what is troubling about prostitution, the fact that the sex worker at least gets money is surely the most defensible part.

With surrogacy, by contrast, it is quite common for people to endorse "gift" or "altruistic" surrogacy while condemning the commercial form. There *are* people who oppose all forms of surrogacy: sometimes on religious grounds, sometimes because it enables gay couples to have children, sometimes because it is thought to encourage people to "play God" and create their children to order. There has been concern that any form of surrogacy undermines the genetic basis of the parent/child relationship and stores up identity problems for children who will not then know who their "real" mother is. Feminists have sometimes argued that encouraging surrogacy arrangements reinforces the idea that childlessness is the worst thing that can happen to a woman, or that the endorsement of altruistic surrogacy relies on and reinforces pressures on women to act in selfless ways and exposes them to exploitative family relationships.[11] There was also a substantial subgroup of feminists in the 1980s who regarded all the new developments in reproductive technology as reckless experimentation on women's bodies by the technocrats of the medical profession.[12] It is not, then, that surrogacy per se is regarded as entirely unproblematic. But whereas with prostitution it makes no sense to separate out judgments of the activity from judgments about whether it should be paid, we can and commonly do make this distinction with surrogacy. Most of the debate focuses on whether or not to condone the development of commercial surrogacy, and jurisdictions that ban markets in surrogacy commonly exempt or leave a loophole for the noncommercial kind.

Surrogate motherhood thus offers a particularly good way of exploring what it is about the commercialisation of a bodily service, that movement from gift to sale, that causes concern. This has not been an easy exploration; this is the chapter that has given me most difficulty, both because my own views have shifted in the course of the research and because the position I ultimately settle on may seem patronising or ignorant to those who have chosen surrogacy. But difficult issues are often the most revealing, and commercial surrogacy provides a challenging case study of the consequences of treating the body—in practice, if not necessarily self-description—as property. If people object, as they commonly do, to descriptions of surrogacy as the "renting out of a womb," are they simply deluding themselves about the nature of the practice? Or does surrogacy differ only in degree from the many occasions on which we receive payment in return for a bodily service, without anyone raising an eyebrow?

The Commodification of Babies

I start by setting aside what some have seen as the most powerful objection to commercial surrogacy: the idea that it turns babies into "things" that can be bought and sold. Surrogacy advocates never, of course, describe it as the sale and purchase of a baby (with occasional exceptions from the world of law and economics, no one defends markets in babies[13]), but the fact that early contracts so decisively linked payment to the delivery of a child gave some credence to this view. As Christine Overall put it, "that the product being sold is the baby itself is most strongly indicated by the fact that if a contract mother changes her mind and refuses to surrender the child, she may not be paid anything at all, let alone the full amount indicated in the contract."[14] Nobody, after all, is paying a woman to get pregnant. They are paying for the delivery of a healthy child. In her study of US surrogacy agencies in the late 1980s and early 1990s, Helena Ragoné observed that agencies were usually keen to dispel this impression and often drew up internal guidelines recommending the payment of monthly instalments throughout the pregnancy, thus a substantial payment even in cases of miscarriage or if the baby was stillborn. However, two out of the eight agencies operating at the time still paid only on delivery of the child.[15]

This kind of payment system is no longer the norm and has been heavily criticised even by advocates of surrogacy.[16] If it were the norm, it still would not establish commercial surrogacy as baby selling, for a system of payment by results is not enough to prove that the product rather than the service is for sale. A teacher paid to prepare a student for an examination, but told the money will only be forthcoming when she has awarded the exam paper a high grade, might well be described as selling, not her professional expertise, but more simply an exam certificate. No pass, no payment: when the contract takes that form, the fact that she might work diligently to impart interesting information looks beside the point, for what is being bought and sold is the grade. But the crucial element in this instance is that this teacher seemingly has the power to determine the student's grade. This is not just any matter of payment by result, but one where the person receiving the payment has the authority to dictate the result. Compare this with the common practice in law firms of pursuing cases for damages on the basis of no win, no fee. Here, too, we see payment dependent on delivery, but unless we assume a totally corrupt legal system, we cannot say that lawyers have the power simply to determine the outcome. They offer this payment system on the basis of a calculation that they will win a sufficiently high proportion of cases to make the loss of the occasional one worthwhile, but there is uncertainty over the outcome, and we cannot fairly describe what they do as "selling" a legal judgment.

A surrogacy contract falls somewhere between these two. The surrogate does not have the power to determine the outcome, for all kinds of things can go wrong in the course of a pregnancy, and one cannot conjure a healthy baby into existence in the same way as one can decide to give a worthless exam paper a high grade. What the woman sells is a service rather than a product, a service without which there would be no baby, but whose outcome she cannot guarantee. The one point at which we could say she has some power to determine the outcome is after the birth, when she may be regretting her agreement to relinquish the child. At this moment, we might say, she gets the money in return for the baby, or keeps the baby and loses the fee. But considering the process as a whole—as seems more sensible—the parallel with the unprofessional teacher selling a grade is not overwhelming. It seems, moreover, to depend on the increasingly rare contracts that pay only on delivery of a healthy child.

I am unconvinced also by the broader argument about surrogacy encouraging us to consider children *as if they were* commodities—a less literal argument than the claim that it is baby selling, and closer to what critics like Elizabeth Anderson or Margaret Radin have suggested.[17] For the brokers, the argument goes, the business of arranging surrogate pregnancies is regulated by the usual business norms. The broker seeks a profit, which means keeping down the costs of the surrogate and keeping up the price. While success is measured by the number of births, the actual children are incidental. For the surrogate, too, we might say the actual children are incidental: they are "valued as mere use-objects," as Anderson puts it, or treated as mere means to someone else's ends.[18] The commissioning parents clearly have an enormous amount invested in the particular child, but *invested* may be the appropriate term, for there is a financial and well as emotional investment, and large sums of money change hands. Critics see the relationship of parents to child as distorted by this intrusion of market norms, with the child carrying through life the burden of living up to its high cost and associated high expectations. "A child who has been specially ordered and paid for by her parent(s) could be treated as an expensive commodity all her life—over-protected, perhaps, or subjected to unreasonably high expectations derived from her high purchase price."[19] The very choice of surrogacy over adoption is sometimes said to indicate the high value prospective parents attach to the child sharing the genetic makeup of at least one of them, and thereby reveals their love as conditional on the child having certain characteristics. That conditionality is further heightened when they specify particular physical or intellectual characteristics for a (nongestational) surrogate, in the hope that these will be passed on to the child.

These are legitimate concerns, though they do not fit particularly well with the way those involved in surrogacy arrangements describe their experiences and feelings. Studies of women acting as surrogates suggest that many take satisfaction out of helping others become parents, and they comment on the joy they may experience when handing over a new son or daughter to the commissioning parents.[20] This does not sound like treating a baby just as a use-value. Studies of those employed in some of the US agencies have emphasised their "exuberant attitude" and the pleasure they get out of helping alleviate the despair of infertile couples.[21] For the commissioning parents, the suggestion that they could have chosen adoption instead of surrogacy does not take seriously enough the complexities of adoption, either for parents or for child. Adoption is not the easy fallback alternative that anyone wanting to be a parent can or ought to pursue: adopted children often find it difficult to deal with their sense of abandonment, and prospective adopters are rightly scrutinised for their suitability for this kind of parenting. The choice of surrogacy may suggest, but does not prove, that parents are simply looking for an extension of themselves.

There *is* an issue, as with all developments in reproductive technology, about the refusal to accept what might previously have been regarded as natural limits, but this is less about commodification and more what Michael Sandel has discussed as the hubris of mastery and control.[22] In the pursuit of genetic and environmental enhancement, wealthy parents sometimes engage in "hyperparenting," seizing the opportunities variously offered by medical science, sports trainers, and educational establishments, to make their children the biggest, the cleverest, and the best. In doing so, they lose the "openness to the unbidden" that Sandel regards as a key component in good parenting: the ability to accept children as who they are rather than transforming them according to a preconceived image. To the extent that surrogacy involves the determined pursuit of children who will carry your genes, it lays itself open to criticism on this score. But whatever the rights and wrongs of this, it cannot be said it amounts to treating children as commodities or babies as things to be bought and sold. The most plausible way to understand commercial surrogacy is not as the purchase and sale of babies, but the purchase and sale of a reproductive service. It is here, in my view, that the problems lie.

Agency: The Wrong Question

I also want to put to one side what I consider the wrong question about whether a surrogate can be assumed to understand what she is committing herself to. Questions about the validity of her consent arose early in commercial surrogacy, in the context of contested cases where the surrogate now wished to keep the child. Courts were initially reluctant to treat the contracts as binding, particularly when the surrogate was the genetic as well as gestational mother. While custody was commonly awarded to commissioning parents, it was typically on the grounds of what were said to be the best interests of the child rather than what the contract said. As gestational surrogacy has increasingly become the norm, however, this pattern has decisively shifted.

Israeli law only allows for gestational surrogacy, and the commissioning parents can claim legal parenthood almost immediately upon birth. In the United States, courts remain reluctant to enforce contracts in which the surrogate is also the genetic mother but are generally unsympathetic to claims by "merely" gestational surrogates, and Florida has legislation explicitly denying parental rights to a gestational surrogate. Recent legislation in India also removes any parental rights for gestational surrogates. In the United Kingdom, by contrast, contracts cannot be enforced and the gestational mother is legally recognised as the mother. This does not mean she can simply claim the child, however, for decisions in contested cases are made, not according to parental rights, but to what are deemed the best interests of the child.

Feminist discourse around the enforceability of surrogacy contracts was to some extent thrown off course by the *Baby M* case, one of the first legal tests of what should happen when a commercial contract breaks down.[23] The initial ruling (in New Jersey in 1987) treated the contract as no different in kind from any other commercial arrangement: the fact that it involved bodies, pregnancy, and babies made no noticeable difference. The court ruled the surrogacy contract binding (though not a clause that would have allowed the commissioning parents to determine whether the surrogate had an abortion), and ordered the gestational, in this case also genetic, mother to relinquish the baby. Mary Beth Whitehead's parental rights were terminated; custody was awarded to William Stern, the genetic father; and his wife was given permission to adopt.

On appeal, the contract was ruled invalid. This was primarily because it conflicted with laws regulating adoption (early jurisprudence on surrogacy tended to treat it as a kind of adoption), but it was also—and significantly—because it was deemed difficult to establish "free and informed consent" in a surrogacy arrangement. The agency of the surrogate was in question. As the appeal judge put it, the surrogate "never makes a totally voluntary informed decision, for quite clearly any decision prior to the baby's birth is, in the most important sense, uninformed, and any decision after that, compelled by a pre-existing contractual commitment, the threat of a lawsuit, and the inducement of a $10,000 payment is less than totally voluntary."[24] The higher court was therefore more sympathetic to the mother's change of heart, though the practical outcome was not so different. The future of M was decided on the basis of the best interests of the child, with custody awarded to the more financially solvent father. Mary Beth Whitehead was, however, recognised as the mother and was granted visitation rights, while Elizabeth Stern was barred from adopting the child.[25]

Most feminists, at the time, were critical of approaches to surrogacy that treated it as no different in kind from any other commercial transaction, but a significant minority argued that relieving women of the obligation to fulfil their contracts encouraged representations of them as weak and feeble creatures.[26] In normal circumstances, it is understood that people can be bound by contract against a later change of mind. It is, in a sense, the whole point of a contract to regulate situations in which people no longer wish to deliver, and contracts that have to be redrawn every time one or the other party has a change of mind hardly seem worth the name. Our sympathies are mostly with the buyer when someone who agrees to sell her car at a particular price later reneges on the agreement, or when the contractor who agreed to rebuild the kitchen decides halfway through that he needs double the money. We may understand why the buyer changed her mind (she realised too late that the car was worth much more), or the contractor doubled the price (he underestimated the cost of the materials), and we may even think the ethical solution is some kind of compromise. But, in general, we think it unfair to renege on contracts involving the exchange of things or the pricing of "normal" labour. Why think any differently about a woman signing a surrogacy contract?

Early positions on this were shaped—I would say mis-shaped—by that second *Baby M* judgment, which made the issue turn too much on whether a woman can be said to know her own mind prior to the pregnancy and childbirth. The suggestion that women are at the mercy of their hormones, or cannot make "a totally voluntary informed decision" when tempted by the offer of $10,000, was seen as particularly outrageous. Marjorie Schultz argued that there was no reason "to presume categorically that women are unable to act freely and responsibly with reference to decisions about procreation and parental intentions";[27] while Carmel Shalev went so far as to suggest that "the free personality of the surrogate mother is nowhere more apparent than when she puts an economic price on her reproductive activity."[28] Imputing to potential surrogates a lack of capacity to make informed decisions, or to women in general a reduced capacity for rational thought, is clearly problematic and at odds with a large body of feminist literature that rejects representations of women as the non-agentic victims, overwhelmed by patriarchal power.[29] The issue here, however, is not whether women lack decision-making capacities or know what they are doing when they sign a surrogacy deal. Let us assume they do. The question is whether in matters involving this kind of use of the body, one can be expected to relinquish the right subsequently to change one's mind.

In the earlier days of the marriage contract, the marriage agreement was understood as including unlimited access to the body for the purposes of sex, and marital rape was deemed an oxymoron. Courts around the world no longer accept that understanding. They recognise, that is, that agreements involving access to a body fall into a different category from agreements regarding detachable bits of property like a car or house. Marriage is not a one-off agreement, referring to a tightly specified period of time, nor is it an agreement the performance of which can be delegated to somebody else (I'm sorry, I can't after all drive you to the airport, but I'll pay for a taxi instead). Marriage is a long-term contract involving the body, and it requires *your* presence, not just anybody's presence, for its fulfilment. This is why the right to divorce is so important, for while we may think people should continue to be bound to a promise to pay us a million dollars even when they no longer find it convenient, this is of a different order from being bound to share someone's life, home, and bed when you no longer love or respect them. The reason we make this distinction is not because we think people are particularly irrational in their marital decisions. People embarking on marriage do often mistake their own interests and desires and frequently make ill-informed decisions, but this is not why societies have come to accept the right to divorce. It is because, in matters so directly involving the body, we must retain the right to change our minds.

The Enforceability of Surrogacy Contracts

At this point, the question arises: what counts as "directly involving the body"? What makes a bodily service "intimate"? What difference does it make if it is? At a commonsense level, it seems evident that paying someone to bear a child is different in kind from paying her to paint your house, but what exactly is the difference? Debra Satz goes through a number of ways in which reproductive labour has been distinguished from other kinds of labour, and notes objections to each. So a contract covering pregnancy covers a nine-month period and involves a long-term commitment. But what about the contracts that commit you to several years of service in the military? So a surrogacy contract is intrusive because of the conditions it imposes on what a woman does with her body during pregnancy. But what about the contracts athletes sign that also commit them to close regulation of diet and exercise (and may imply, if not officially include, provisions regulating when they have sex)? So the capacity to reproduce is closely bound up with a woman's sense of identity and should not therefore be available for sale. But what about rabbis and priests, whose sense of identity is presumably very much bound up with their religious commitments, but who nonetheless accept payment for performing religious services?[30] Critiques of commercial surrogacy often depend on what Satz regards as essentialised understandings of reproductive labour. Sometimes they invoke downright romantic ones, showing no awareness of the difficulties many women experience with pregnancy or the extent of postnatal depression. Claims about the specialness of pregnancy are particularly problematic for those of us who would like to see less focus on the genetic basis for parenting and want to see the responsibility for child care shared equally between women and men. These scenarios are not promoted by discourses that naturalise the relationship between mother and fetus/child.

In Elizabeth Anderson's critique of commercial surrogacy, she does not claim that pregnant women come "naturally" to love their child and distances herself from biologically based arguments about what they are likely to feel. She stresses, however, that the social practices of pregnancy are mostly organised so as to facilitate a mother/child bond. The pregnancy of the surrogate is, on this account, alienated (this is the term she uses) "because she must divert it from the end which the social practices of pregnancy rightly promote—an emotional bond with her child." In her early writings on surrogacy, Mary Shanley stresses the fluidity of the boundary between self and other, and the damage a pregnant woman can do to her sense of who she is when required to think of herself as simply doing a job. Shanley is sensitive to the point about us carrying the body with us in everything we do, and the implication that all labour contracts—not just those associated with "intimacy"—imply the provision of a bodily service. She claims, however, that "the forfeiture of self involved in contract pregnancy is an *extreme instance* [my emphasis] of the diminution of the self involved in many labor contracts."[31] Although more nuanced than accusations of essentialism suggest, these accounts lay themselves open to criticism as making pregnancy too special. Yet I read Shanley, in particular, as making a point about differences of degree rather than kind, certainly not as saying we should worry about the risk to selfhood in contract pregnancy but not the risks to selfhood in contract anything else. Surrogacy reveals to us a truth about all kinds of work: it is, as she puts it, an "extreme instance" of what we risk in any kind of labour. All employment contracts transfer elements of our authority over our bodies to those who employ us, and while the consequences of this transfer are minimal in some jobs and maximal in others, it is important to recognise the continuum.

It is also worth stressing that the *general* notion of bodies as different is widely recognised in law. If someone reneges on a contract to sell a house or hand over some preagreed sum, the courts will typically order the reluctant party to fulfil the contract and deliver the property in question. If she reneges, however, on a contract to perform certain services (to do things, that is, with her body), the courts do not normally order what is described as specific performance, preferring to award monetary compensation instead. And this is not something restricted to especially "intimate" services. Requiring a domestic servant to serve out her contract with an employer she can no longer bear, or a singer to complete her contract with a recording company when she has definitively fallen out with her producer, is also felt to be too much like slavery. Ordering us to deliver property is one thing. Ordering specific performance is seen as involving too much personal subordination.

As regards the enforceability of surrogacy contracts, this general recognition of the body as different already makes it illegitimate to enforce the often highly intrusive conditions attached to surrogacy arrangements (and would make it illegitimate to enforce a prostitution contract, should any client have the nerve to take his case to court). Surrogacy contracts have included clauses banning alcohol consumption, sex with one's partner, and otherwise regulating diet and lifestyle. They have required the pregnant woman to undergo a battery of medical tests, including amniocentesis. They have included clauses forbidding her to seek, or in cases of foetal injury, requiring her to have, an abortion. In the highly regulated Israeli contracts, the woman typically agrees to refrain from smoking, drinking, or sex during the pregnancy; to receive daily hormone injections at the beginning, and take all required tests, medicines, and vitamin supplements during the pregnancy; and to undergo selective reduction of the embryos, caesarean birth, or intrauterine foetal surgery, as considered necessary by the doctors. In the Indian surrogacy hostels, the surrogates move, for the period of their pregnancy, into rooms at the IVF clinic or nearby hostels, and their daily routine is regulated by a system of rules and regular injections. If a woman backtracks on any of these agreements, she can expect to lose some, if not all, of her fee, but it is hard to envisage a court ordering her to do what she promised to do. Think, indeed, of what would be involved in making someone either have or refrain from having sex against her will, or in forcing her into an operating theatre for a procedure she has refused. That the body is *intimately* involved may or may not be relevant, but just the fact that the *body* is involved is already understood as making a difference.

Advocates of enforceability typically accept this point but stress that it does not extend to the central issue of enforceability, which is whether a woman can be required to relinquish a child. Requiring this is said to escape the ban on specific performance because the baby is separable from the woman. As Marjorie Schultz put it, "an order to surrender the child does not directly control the promisor's own body, time, services, selfhood in quite the way [as] compelled performance of a personal service against one's will."[32]

From *Baby M* onwards, this is the point those troubled by surrogacy have found hardest to swallow. Many have been swayed by the arguments about women having the right to do as they choose with their bodies, and what seems the inconsistency in banning the exchange of money for reproductive services when we permit the exchange of money for so much else. But the idea that a woman who has just given birth to a child can be required, by law, to relinquish the baby, is often the breaking point. One common position on commercial surrogacy therefore rejects the idea of enforceable contracts while remaining agnostic on the validity of commercial surrogacy per se. This is an especially attractive position if you share the view that it is difficult to specify why women should not be permitted to market their reproductive services in much the same way as they market their domestic or office or sales services and are sensitive to the evidence that many surrogates appear happy with their job. Taking a stand only against that final enforceability allows you to offer protection to the most obviously vulnerable (the women who come, in the course of their pregnancy, to regret the agreement to relinquish the child), while still accepting the agency and self-description of the others who do not recognise themselves in depictions of surrogacy as alienation or diminution. If the vast majority of surrogates are happy with their arrangements, so be it. But let's at least ensure that a surrogate mother who later changes her mind does not have to relinquish the child.

This middle position is not, of course, particularly attractive to the agencies, whose marketing becomes more difficult if they cannot guarantee delivery. It is not particularly safe ground, even, for the surrogate, for if the contract cannot be enforced against *her* later wishes, it presumably cannot be enforced if the commissioning parents change *their* minds. (This has happened on a number of occasions, either because their relationship fell into difficulties or because the child was born with some unwanted disability.) The commissioning parents can also be said to get a raw deal, for they make a large emotional investment in becoming parents and will not know until long into the process whether the child will ultimately be theirs. Given the uncertainties attached to any pregnancy, this is not a unique experience; it is certainly not so different from the experience of those adopting babies, who normally wait a considerable period after the birth not knowing whether the birth mother will finally sign the papers. But if we think that people have some right to control what happens to their reproductive material, then those who provide the ovum and sperm do have a claim, both on their own behalf and that of the child. It is hard to face the possibility that a child sharing many of your attributes is to be parented, against your wishes, by someone else, and it may, at some later stage, be hard for the child. We know, from the experiences of adopted children, that the sense of genetic connection can matter a great deal. Even if this is a cultural artefact, and not something that affects everyone equally, that does not make it unimportant.

Despite these problems, I have often come close to endorsing the middle position, but I do not in the end find it compelling. My reasons for this relate not so much to the difficulties in balancing the anguish of the surrogate against the anguish of the commissioning parents, but refer back to my earlier argument about needing to look, not just at the beginning and end of a process, but what happens in between. I have said that the real drama of most work situations begins after the contract has been signed, as employers seek to exert their authority over those whose services they have engaged, and employees have to accept, negotiate, or resist demands whose full content may only become apparent at that stage. The parallel with surrogacy may look strained, for the "employers" in this case cannot exert much authority (think of those restrictions on ordering specific performance), and most of the work of the surrogate takes place in the privacy of her own home. But the general point still applies: it is a mistake to think that the only or main problem with commercial surrogacy is that it forces some women, against their later wishes, to relinquish a child. What happens *during* the process is equally, if not more, disturbing.

Any paid employment requires things of the body and exposes it to risk (as both Shanley and Satz observe, there are plenty of labour contracts that do this), but the exposure associated with prostitution and the regulation associated with commercial surrogacy far exceed the norm. Sex workers commonly set conditions in their arrangements with clients: no sex without a condom, for example, or no anal sex, or no kissing. Much of the danger of their work is that these arrangements may not be honoured: the contract is not like handing over a piece of property for money, but temporarily at least, putting yourself in someone else's power. With commercial surrogacy, "employer" breaches of the initial agreement are less of a risk. The problem here is the often-extreme regulation of the body and the associated regulation of the mind. As Elizabeth Anderson stresses, commercial pregnancy requires pregnant women to manage their emotions in ways that will minimise the development of a mother/child bond. What strikes me forcibly in the accounts of commercial surrogacy is the effort that goes into the management and manipulation of these emotions, the effort that goes into ensuring that women do *not* change their minds.

Surrogates do not necessarily object to this management; they are more likely, indeed, to object to descriptions of themselves as alienated or anguished than to the manipulation of their bodies and feelings. But not objecting cannot, in this context, be taken as conclusive evidence, for the descriptions we give of ourselves do not simply reveal what we feel. They also reveal what we want or need to feel, and they often express ambiguities and tensions. This seems very much the case with the narratives women provide in talking of decisions to become a surrogate mother, or decisions to become a commissioning parent. The commodity aspects of the trade are softened by reference to the "gift of life," as if nothing so crude as money changes hands; the right to sell one's reproductive services is *not* defended in a discourse of self-ownership, and the body *not* described as property; and even the global hierarchies and inequalities are reduced by discourses about helping those less fortunate. Lisa Ikemoto quotes one surrogacy client explaining the decision to travel from the United Kingdom to India in these terms: "You cannot ignore the discrepancies between Indian poverty and

Western wealth. . . . We try our best not to abuse this power. Part of our choice to come here was the idea that there was an opportunity to help someone in India."[33] I do not describe these discourses simply as self-deception, but the very compulsion to find alternative narratives reveals something of the difficulties of the work.

In her interviews with Israeli surrogates, Elly Teman found no particular resistance to the demanding requirements imposed on them, but almost a welcoming of the medical manipulation as helping secure the necessary distance that enabled them to do the work. One woman talked of the "stranger" hormones injected into her system. In Teman's analysis, she used these "as conceptual pawns to help her disembody and depersonalize the pregnancy."[34] As required by Israeli law, all the surrogates already had a child or children of their own, and all differentiated strongly between how they had experienced their own "natural" pregnancies and their experience of the "artificial" pregnancy of surrogacy. All insisted that the baby they were carrying was in no sense theirs. Given that they had virtually no chance of claiming the baby as their own, but were required to deliver it to the commissioning parents in the presence of a welfare officer as soon as possible after the birth, these highly developed distancing mechanisms were almost a necessity.

In the United States, agencies have operated in arguably more benign way to achieve the same effect. Surrogacy arrangements commonly operate on an open model, with commissioning parents encouraged to build up relationships with the surrogate and maintain contact through the pregnancy. One might defend this on humane grounds alone, but the open model also turns out to be a good way of minimising contested cases. Certainly, in Helena Ragoné's early study, contested cases were a more common phenomenon in agencies that treated surrogacy more starkly as a business transaction.[35] In those agencies, the anonymity of the commissioning parents was carefully guarded, and the surrogates had little contact. In the open model, by contrast, they had a constant reminder of the commissioning parents' despair at their infertility and excitement at the prospect of parenthood, and they were encouraged to bond with the couple rather than the baby. As the director of one programme put it: "The surrogate bonds with the couple and not the baby; when the surrogate gives up the baby, she doesn't feel separation anxiety from giving up the baby but from losing her couple."[36] Ragoné notes a number of occasions when surrogates expressed disappointment that what they had considered a genuine friendship with the commissioning parents came to an abrupt end after the baby was born.[37]

Examples like this suggest that it is hard for surrogates to sustain the necessary distance, and that much of the work of the agencies goes into managing the experience so as to produce their desired result. Although the number of contested cases is small, surrogates do still find it difficult to relinquish a child. COTS, one of the non-profit-making agencies in the United Kingdom, reports that 2 percent of surrogates decide to keep the child, and it seems reasonable to assume that more than this find themselves troubled at the end of the pregnancy. A commercial agency cannot afford to leave it at that, but will try to regulate the process so as to minimise potential contestations and maximise the ease of handover. In Pande's study of surrogacy in India, "the surrogates are periodically told that their role is only as a vessel, that they have no genetic connection with the baby, and that it will be taken away from them immediately after delivery."[38] Although they resist these narratives in various ways, for example, by stressing their special relationship to the intending couple, the repeated reminders are mostly effective in ensuring that babies are handed over with minimal fuss. The management of the emotions is not peculiar to commercial surrogacy; as the work of Arlie Hochschild and others has demonstrated, there are many forms of employment in which this now plays a significant part.[39] But the work that goes into managing the emotions of commercial surrogacy, and the very *non*commercial narratives those most involved in the trade tend to provide, do mark it out as distinctive.

The commercialism of surrogacy brings with it—requires of its participants—a distancing and disembodiment that is, in Mary Shanley's words, a more "extreme instance" of the distancing we all engage in when we do not feel able to throw ourselves wholeheartedly into our work. It is distinctive though not unique; it is not unique even to activities that directly involve the body. In a world of self-owners, where the only consideration is whether surrogates have freely chosen their work, one might be hard put to come up with any compelling objection. But if one believes (as I do) that the acceptability of activities rests on more than whether there are people willing to do them, it is not just a question of whether people know what they are letting themselves in for, or freely accept the conditions. Objections to child labour do not stand or fall by evidence that the children are unwilling to do it, for we can plausibly argue that their physical and intellectual development is being stunted, even when they feel entirely happy in the work. To switch the example to fully agentic adults, the fact that some people are willing, even eager, to work in conditions others consider too dangerous does not, of itself, sweep away the objections. Where employment legislation sets minimum safety requirements, it is not up to the self-owning individuals alone to decide whether or not to comply. There are responsibilities on the part of the society to protect even fully agentic individuals from danger (as when legislation requires everyone to wear seat belts when driving), and since the choices of one individual can alter the choice-set for others (as when the willingness of some to work long hours of overtime makes it hard for others to refuse), even freely chosen work can be legitimately banned.

The deep implication of body and emotions in the service provided by surrogates does not put it decisively on the other side of a "prophylactic line," but does place it on the further edge of a continuum, where the regulation of body and emotions reaches particularly troubling levels. That regulation, moreover, is exclusively directed at women, and Debra Satz makes this point a centrepiece in her own reservations regarding commercial surrogacy. Surrogacy places women's bodies, and *only women's bodies*, under the control of others, and this asymmetry can work to perpetuate gender inequality. In Satz's argument, "the problem with commodifying women's reproductive labor is not that it degrades the special nature of reproductive labor or alienates women from a core part of their identities, but that it reinforces (to the extent that it does) a traditional gender-hierarchical division of labor."[40] If commercial surrogacy becomes widespread—if it continues to develop in the almost factory direction that characterises the sector in India or Thailand—it could work to reinforce stereotypes about women as "baby machines."

Sales, Gifts, and Recompense

In my discussion so far I have talked of commercial surrogacy as if there were a straightforward distinction between this and the "altruistic" type. Yet the countries that ban the first while permitting the second (these currently include the United Kingdom, Australia, and Canada) typically tolerate the existence of non-profit-making matching agencies and allow the payment of "reasonable" expenses. The distinction between the two regimes then becomes somewhat murky. Canada's Assisted Human Reproduction Act (2004) makes it a criminal offence to pay a woman to be a surrogate but permits reimbursement for expenses; uncertainty about what exactly is permitted has meant that Canadian couples often prefer to cross the border to those US states that allow overtly commercial arrangements. In the United Kingdom, The Surrogacy Arrangements Act (1985) combines with The Human Fertilization and Embryology Act (1990) to ban commercial surrogacy and make it a criminal offence to advertise for surrogate mothers. Non-profitmaking matching agencies are, however, permitted to operate, using websites to bring together potential surrogates and couples, charging "membership fees" for their service, and helping set up arrangements in which surrogates are paid "reasonable expenses." Lawyers are rarely involved in drafting the agreements; the surrogate is treated in law as the mother, whether she is genetically so or not, and as is the practice with adoption, cannot finally consent to relinquishing the child until at least six weeks after the birth. Mechanisms have, however, developed to enable surrogacy arrangements, the most important of which is that when the intending father's name is put on the birth certificate (this is at the discretion of the surrogate), he is recognised as having equal parental rights, and rather than going through a lengthy facsimile of the adoption process, the intending parents can apply after six weeks for a parental order.

"Altruistic" surrogacy conjures up images of women helping infertile relatives or friends, but most surrogacy arrangements in the United Kingdom are between people previously unknown to one another, with substantial amounts of money changing hands. Although evidence of large payments should, according to the law, nullify an arrangement, the courts have been unwilling to implement this, preferring to settle custody arrangements according to what they see as in the best interests of the child. Typical payments had reached £10,000 to £15,000 by the end of the 1990s—not so different, then, from the sums paid in explicitly commercial markets in parts of the United States. What sense can we make of this? If surrogacy is problematic, does that not extend equally to "altruistic" arrangements? Alternatively, if the "noncommercial" arrangements are legitimate, on what basis could one object to the more overtly commercial ones?

In his work on the gift relationship, Richard Titmuss argued that a society in which people are willing to give blood to assist unknown strangers is better than one in which they will only sell their blood for money, and that permitting a market in blood promotes self-interest at the expense of altruistic motives.[41] I am sympathetic to his argument, particularly where the work of donation is relatively undemanding, as in giving semen or blood. But while the donation of blood might reasonably be regarded as a civic duty, few would think that women had a moral or civic duty to undergo the physically and emotionally draining pregnancy of a surrogate mother. When the act itself is so much beyond what most women will offer to do, can it be appropriate nonetheless to refuse compensation? When it is, further, something that only one sex can do, it is hard not to share Marjorie Schultz's irritation that the commodification objection to paying surrogates "smacks all too familiarly of the notion that while men get paid for their efforts, skills and services, women, being women, should do their woman-things out of purity of heart and sentiment."[42]

Egg donors sometimes say they would welcome the offer of compensation even when they would refuse it, because they would see this as recognising the significance of their donation. With surrogates, the case seems even more compelling: one would expect, at a minimum, to compensate a surrogate for out-of-pocket expenses, special foods, visits to the doctor, babysitting costs, and loss of earnings. Beyond these, pregnancy is hard and childbirth appropriately termed labour, and however rewarding and life changing the experience of pregnancy can be, it still involves physical discomfort, risk, restrictions on mobility, and pain. It would be difficult to justify an intending couple receiving these simply as a gift, without offering any compensation. It is hard to justify even in the (rare) cases in which the surrogate is a relative or friend: one would imagine people wanting to show their appreciation somehow, if only by offering to fund a holiday. To be consistent, societies should either ban surrogacy altogether (which I would see as an unjustifiable restriction on autonomy), allow it only between close relatives and friends (which can bring its own problems as regards the child's sense of identity), or accept that a woman agreeing to bear a child for someone else is entitled to some recompense. If surrogacy arrangements of any kind are permitted, it is exploitative not to recognise the work involved and offer some reward.

We should regard this, however, as compensation rather than payment: compensation for actual costs, combined perhaps with some monetary recognition of the generosity of the donor, but not a market-driven payment reflecting overall supply and demand. This may appear an academic distinction, but it is important to separate out whether it is fair to ask people to do something for nothing from whether it is appropriate to introduce a market. Payment is not the same as a market, and sometimes, as Donna Dickenson puts it, " 'to pay or not to pay' isn't the question."[43] If I pay one of my sons to mow the lawn, I might regret, Titmuss style, that he did not offer to do it for love and reflect rather sourly on the transaction as evidence of the increased monetarisation of human relationships, but it cannot be said that I have introduced a market. There have to be more than two individuals involved before one can sensibly talk of a market, and it is not a market unless open to buyers and sellers with whom I have no familial connection. The suggestion here is that it is possible to agree to a system of compensation without committing oneself to the introduction of a market, and that the case for the first does not determine positions on the second.

The incoherence of legal regimes that ban commercial surrogacy yet permit substantial "compensatory" payments begins to dissolve once one recognises that the object is to discourage the development of markets in reproductive services and careers in surrogate motherhood, while resisting the criminalization of surrogacy and permitting reasonable "compensation." It remains anomalous that payments to the surrogate should end up much the same in commercial and "noncommercial" systems, but the principle underpinning the regime is coherent enough. It recognizes that pregnancy is work, but it seeks to prevent profiteering from surrogacy arrangements and limits (though it cannot entirely eliminate) the development of a market. While I continue to think there is something slippery about banning commercial surrogacy while permitting commercial rates of pay, the important distinction underpinning this is that between marketisation and payment. This is a distinction that makes a difference.

Consider, in the light of this, a proposal made by Mary Shanley and Sujatha Jesudason in a recent paper on surrogacy. They propose a regulatory regime, informed by practices in adoption, that would enable children born through surrogacy to learn the identity of the surrogate and any gamete provider, thereby avoiding what one participant terms "donor-and-surrogacy amnesia," and facilitating the formation of new family relationships between parents, surrogates, and child.[44] That kind of development would be entirely compatible with the payment of compensation—even significant levels of compensation—to surrogates. I cannot imagine it being adopted by profit-making agencies in the global surrogacy market.

The question is not whether a woman should receive anything in return for the nine months' labour of her pregnancy, undertaken in order to provide a child for someone else. I see no basis for refusing compensation for such a major commitment, or for refusing to provide this in the form of money and limiting it to payment in kind. With surrogacy, the key issue is not the commodification of babies, or whether the surrogate knows what she is doing when she enters the contract, or whether she is entitled to some financial reward. The problem is that when surrogacy is put in an explicitly commercial context, this shapes the practices and relationships in potentially damaging ways. That surrogates steer so resolutely clear of the language of property and self-ownership is, in my view, an important feature of the experience. To repeat an earlier point, the widespread discomfort with the language of body property among those whose activities might otherwise seem to endorse it is a significant indictment.

CHAPTER FOUR

Spare Parts and Desperate Need

THE PREVIOUS CHAPTER DEALT with commercialised practices in which claims to the ownership of one's body play surprisingly little part. Surrogates either stress the "gift" aspect of the activity, playing down the commercial exchange, or emphasise the economic necessity that drove them to engage in it, playing down those elements of choice and personal control usually associated with property claims. With body parts and tissues, we encounter further twists to the tale. There is growing pressure for countries to accept markets in bodily materials as a normal part of life, and some argue for this in the terms noted in chapter one: "*because* [my emphasis] you own yourself and your labour, you must have the right to use your body and labour in any way you see fit consistent with the rights of others. So, if you want to sell your sexual services, you have a right to do so. If you want to sell your organs, you should be free to do so. If you want to take recreational drugs, it's your mind and body to do with as you see fit."[1] Others, however, rely on utilitarian arguments that centre on the desperate need of those waiting for organ transplants, and some of these actively contest more individualised property claims. Those, moreover, who see the less powerful as needing better protection against commercial exploitation often frame this call in property terms.

The debate is far from academic, for body parts and tissues now have unprecedented use value. With the success of complex transplant operations, body parts previously of no use to anyone but oneself—heart, kidneys, liver, lungs, corneas, even the face—can transform and save the lives of others. Developments in assisted reproduction not only enable the growth of commercial surrogacy but also much increase the use of "donor" gametes. Stem cell research currently depends on supplies of human eggs. Skin grafting techniques for the treatment of burn victims depend on large supplies of human skin. So, too, does cosmetic surgery. Blood samples taken for diagnostic purposes and body tissue excised during operations—materials previously discarded as waste—are now important resources for medical research and are stored in tissue banks for the study of illness. Writing in 2001, Lori Andrews and Dorothy Nelkin reported that there were already over 282 million pathological specimens stored in US repositories, with at least 20 million new specimens being added each year.[2] What is more, they noted, "the language of science is increasingly permeated with the commercial language of supply and demand, contracts, exchange, and compensation. Body parts are *extracted* like a mineral, *harvested* like a crop, or *mined* like a resource. Tissue is *procured*—a term more commonly used for land, goods and prostitutes."[3] Writing in the same year about markets in gametes, embryos, and body tissues, Suzanne Holland claimed that "we are witnessing nothing less than a new kind of gold rush, and the territory is the body."[4] There is now a huge demand—and market—for body tissues and parts. That language of gold rush is widely deployed.

Although the scale is unprecedented, markets in bodies and body parts are not entirely novel. Corpses have been employed in the training of doctors for centuries, often sourced from the bodies of executed criminals or the unclaimed bodies of those dying in penury. As the number of doctors increased, university medical schools began to supplement their legal sources with cadavers stolen from graves. In the infamous Burke and Hare case, people were even murdered for the sake of their bodies.[5] Murder has always been considered shocking, and murder for profit particularly so. Nowadays, most of us would also object to the appropriation of the bodies of the poor and criminal. This is not because people are now regarded, but were not then, as owning their bodies, or as now having, but not then, the right to refuse the use of their cadaver in medical training. The more significant cultural shift has been the permeation of ideas of human equality, which make it illegitimate to employ the bodies of criminals or the destitute in ways we would not countenance for ourselves.[6] The idea that a body becomes available for pillaging just because the person who died lacked status or wealth would now (or at least, *should* now) be considered at odds with the most minimal principles of democracy or human rights. If cadavers are to be used in this way, this should be done without discrimination.

So far as live body parts are concerned, the main precursor of today's demand is blood, which has been collected and stored in blood banks since the 1930s for use in transfusions. Some of the issues associated with the transformation of human bodies into collections of marketable parts are anticipated in the discussion of blood supplies, and particularly in the debate between those who advocate payment for blood and those who favour altruistic donation. From Titmuss's *The Gift Relationship* onwards, decisions about whether to pay blood donors have been seen as involving more than a calculation of which system produces the better supply.[7] This is not just a matter of weighing the relative efficiency of donation versus sale: of balancing out the respective costs to the hospital, or the risk that too few will be inspired to give against the danger that those seeking payment will be disproportionately poor, addicted, or desperate, therefore more tempted to conceal medically important information. There *are* issues here, though improved screening techniques reduce the reliance on information actively volunteered about medical history and make worries about contaminated supplies less of a concern. When donation proves inadequate, moreover, hospitals may still have to buy in blood from countries operating a payment system, so the practical differences may not be that great.

The larger issue Titmuss addresses is that introducing a system of payment for blood could undermine the willingness of those who otherwise donate. In reducing the practice of altruism in one sphere, this could contribute to a general lessening of gift relationships. It is hard to test this out: Cécile Fabre observes that there is not much difference in the proportion of people giving blood in the United States, where they could seek payment instead, and the United Kingdom, where sales are not permitted, but given the many factors at work, the comparison is not decisive.[8] What we can say is that the kind of calculation that goes into deciding whether to sell something is very different from that which goes into deciding whether to give. Indeed, if it isn't different—if people calculate in exactly the same way, checking out whether the value of what they give will be equivalent to what they receive in return, and doing their best to ensure it is neither more nor less—we are inclined to see this as at odds with the very spirit of giving.[9] If we value gift relationships, as I think we should, then we are surely right to worry about whether creeping commercialisation undermines them.

In the previous chapter I argued that it would be unfair to accept the services of a surrogate simply as gift, without ensuring she is no worse off as a result. In that context I also suggested that the language of altruism can operate as a way of managing emotions, keeping the surrogate's mind fixed on what she is "giving" to the commissioning couple and away from her own potentially troubling relationship to the foetus. The distinction I made there was between donation with reasonable compensation and a commercial sale. Nine months' pregnancy is a major commitment, and once surrogacy arrangements move beyond the close network of family and friends—once surrogates are assisting strangers with their infertility problems—donation with no compensation looks distinctly unfair. Such arrangements lack reciprocity, with all the benefits loaded on one side and all the risks on the other. Even allowing for the sense of satisfaction many surrogates say they take from their work, this is far outweighed by the benefits to the commissioning couple. Whatever their feelings of gratitude to the surrogate, they are using her for their own purposes (to have a family) while she does the work out of the generosity of her heart. Even gift relationships are supposed to involve some kind of reciprocity. Calculating precise returns on a present is at odds with the spirit of giving, but so too is accepting a gift without feeling any need to reciprocate.

I have argued, then, that if surrogacy is to be permitted beyond the close network of family and friends, it should be compensated, and not just that it is legitimate to offer compensation but that it would be unfair not to do so. So what, if anything, does this imply about compensation for body products and parts? The main "compensation" blood donors get in the United Kingdom is a cup of hot sweet tea. Do I think this, too, an unfair arrangement, with recipients of the blood getting a life and donors just biscuits and tea? I am, in fact, with Titmuss on this, and my different approach to questions of surrogacy and blood donation derives from three considerations. First, giving blood is a much less demanding activity than bearing a child; second, it is something both sexes can do; third, it is an inherently reciprocal activity in that all of us may at some point need a blood transfusion. The first point is pretty straightforward, though it is worth noting (I shall return to this) that people neither seek nor accept compensation for kidney donation, even though that process is closer in its intrusiveness to surrogacy than blood donation. The point about both sexes being able to give blood but only women acting as surrogates matters because of the shadow it casts over appeals to altruism. When only one group can provide a service, this necessarily changes the dynamic. It is one thing to represent something as gift or civic duty when we can all be expected to contribute, but quite another to do so when only some are in a position to give. As regards abortion, feminists have sometimes noted that a ban on legal abortion imposes on women—but *only* women—the responsibility for bringing a foetus to full term, and they have argued that this inequality between the sexes is the fundamental reason why women must retain the right to choose. As regards surrogacy, that inequality certainly rules out thinking of it as a civic duty but also makes it difficult to justify as gift.

The third point of distinction is that those seeking surrogacy arrangements are themselves a subgroup: people with fertility problems, who want children, and care that those children are genetically related to them. This further undercuts the reciprocity in these arrangements. Titmuss noted that the gift of blood is a particularly unusual one, in that the giver neither expects nor wants (since we would prefer never to need it) a corresponding gift in return. That said, reciprocity remains at the heart of the donation. We can all give blood, and while we may hope to avoid the eventuality, each of us may at some point become recipients. By contrast, a good half of us (men) can never act as surrogates, and the vast majority of us will never "need" a surrogacy arrangement.

What, however, of those who donate sperm and ova in the confident belief that they need never be on the receiving end, or those who undergo the major operation required to extract a spare kidney? It would also be odd to think of these activities as part of one's civic duty (though Fabre comes close to this when she argues that justice can imply the mandatory transfer of body parts). The main issue here has been whether to offer compensation to donors, and if so, at what level, and more radically, whether to take the further step towards markets in body parts. With human gametes, opinion (and legislation) currently varies between offering some relatively token compensation and permitting profit-making commercial trade. With human organs, the commercial option is strongly frowned upon, and governments around the world have passed legislation to make it illegal to trade in live human organs. In the United Kingdom, evidence that people were travelling to Britain to sell their kidneys prompted the 1989 Human Organ Transplant Act, which made it illegal to make or receive payment for the supply of human organs. In India, revelations about the nature and scale of the market in kidneys prompted the 1994 Transplantation of Human Organs Act, which bans their sale and requires transplant centres to establish that any nonrelated living donors are acting out of "affection or attachment," not for payment. (This is relatively easy to circumvent. Given the pressures that can be exerted within families on poorer relatives, there is no guarantee that even donors related to the recipient will be acting out of affection.) China also had a thriving trade in human organs through the 1990s, but scandals about nonconsensual harvesting and deaths after the extraction of organs prompted a ban in 2006. With few exceptions, there is currently a global consensus that human organs should not be treated as tradable commodities. Even in Iran, where payment for organs is legal, the money is described, not as payment, but as a "social" or "sacrifice gift."[10] Since altruistic donation falls considerably short of the demand, however, there is a significant body of opinion arguing that we need markets to meet the need.[11]

In what I have written so far, I have been concerned with the application of ownership models to the body. I have argued that when we start to attach an explicitly property significance to our use of the possessive adjective, we minimise the significance of our bodies to our sense of self and encourage a mind/body dualism that makes it easier to think of bodies as marketable resources. There is no inevitability to this chain of consequences, but recognisable ways in which property claims go along with objectification, objectification enables commodification, commodification enables exploitation, and all potentially link together in the development of commercial markets. I have stressed, however, that the connections are by no means straightforward. Formulating rape as an offence against property makes us neither more nor less likely to favour the commodification of the body, while those involved in commercial surrogacy often object strongly to the designation of their activities as the renting out of the body. In the case of body products and parts, we find a further confounding of expectations, for the language of property and property rights is here invoked, not only by advocates of a market, but also by those most opposed to it. If we are to stop the "gold rush" for bodies and body parts, it is frequently argued, we may need stronger assertions of ownership in the body, not weaker.

Commenting on debates about the market in body tissues, Roger Brownsword identifies three broad positions: a utilitarian perspective that focuses on overall benefits to human welfare, a human rights view that insists on our right to control the uses made of our bodies and body products, and what he terms a "dignitarian" view that sees any trade in body tissues as at odds with human dignity.[12] Property rights figure mainly in the arguments of the second group, as part of the armoury, that is, of those challenging rapid commercialisation. There is a similar pattern in the literature on body products and parts. The typical argument in favour of a market is that selling unused or renewable body products (spare kidneys or eggs, renewable sperm or blood) has no significant impact on our sense of self yet brings enormous benefits to those in need. There is no great cost, that is, to either the source or society in general, while the benefits of the trade to the sick, dying, and infertile are beyond doubt. The argument often involves some kind of mind/body dualism (as when Julian Savulescu says "I am my mind"[13]), and typically applies a language of resources—by implication, therefore, of property—to the body. But the underlying ethic is utilitarian, and the notion of property rights carries no special weight. John Harris, for example, has been a strong advocate of regulated markets in kidneys, but not because he thinks our bodies belong to us and we should therefore be free to do what we like with them. His central concern has been that without markets, many people suffering from kidney disease will die.[14] Since he also regards us as under a moral obligation to support and participate in research that brings benefits to humankind, he does not think we should be entitled to refuse consent for the use of excised tissue (removed, for example, during an operation) just because the likely research use is something we personally disapprove of or see as irrelevant to ourselves.[15] He would have little sympathy for the person who went around insisting that her pathological specimens belonged to her, that they had been stored without her consent, and that she wanted them removed from the data bank because she did not trust the researchers to behave in an ethical way.

There is a particular challenge then, in the arguments about body tissues and parts, for many who share my concerns about the transformation of the human body into bits and pieces of profitable material do not share my focus on body property as an important part of the problem. For these critics (some of whom fall into what Brownsword terms the *human rights camp*), property, objectification, commodification, and exploitation are *not* linked together in an even roughly likely chain, and property emerges more as ally than threat. Some of these arguments resonate with my own teasing apart of monetary compensation and markets in the last chapter; others I find less convincing. I address them more directly later in the chapter. For the moment, I turn to the most contentious of the body part issues: the case for and against markets in live human organs like kidneys.

Markets in Kidneys

There already are markets in kidneys. Payment to nonrelated donors is legal in a small number of countries, including Iran, but there is also illicit harvesting of kidneys, with scandals periodically reported in the media, as well as unknown numbers of supposedly altruistic donors who are in fact being paid. The World Health Organization estimates that as many as 10 percent of the sixty thousand plus kidney transplants carried out each year involve payment to a nonrelated donor. The more illegal and undercover this trade, the more risk there is of suppliers being deceived about the risks, cheated of their payments, or dying from bungled operations.[16] The desperate need in the kidney trade is twofold: the desperate need of those suffering kidney failure, and facing a reduced life on dialysis or early death, and the desperate need of those who decide to sell. But some of the worst excesses can be traced to the fact that the trade is illegal, hence covert. Given the risks to vendors, and the significant number of patients dying each year while waiting for a transplant, why not make the transactions more open? Why not allow people to sell nonvital parts of their body while they are still alive? If we allow them to donate, we presumably do not consider the health risks prohibitive. Why not also allow them to sell?

The standard answer is *commodification* and *exploitation*, the point at issue not being whether these are good things but whether the terms sensibly apply to a market in body parts. Treating human beings as commodities is clearly indefensible. Commodities are goods that are traded, and no one now defends a trade in human beings. The charge of exploitation is trickier, for there are normatively neutral meanings of exploitation (it is not self-evidently wrong to exploit a situation, for example, so long as you are not also exploiting a person), and much then depends on what people mean by the term. In general, however, everyone agrees that human beings should not be treated as objects or commodities and thinks it a bad state of affairs when they are exploited. The question is whether the sale of body parts brings about either of these states of affairs.

Although I have noted that objectification and commodification are not the same, I shall treat them in this context as pretty much interchangeable, for while services can be commodified without becoming objects, and people can be treated in object-like fashion without being available for sale, worries about the commodification of body parts are basically worries about treating parts of the body, and by extension, the person, as marketable things. They reflect, that is, Margaret Radin's dual understanding of commodification as coming to view parts of a person as if they were "possessions bearing a value characterizeable in money terms" and "objects separate from the self."[17] Two questions then arise. Does paying for a body part necessarily mean treating it like a commodity, as "characterizeable in money terms" and "separate from the self"? And if it does, is the body part sufficiently integral to what it means to be human for its sale to mean the person is being treated as a commodity too? The main line of defence on the first count has been that money combines with many other meanings, so the mere fact that money changes hands does not of itself make something a commodity. The main defence on the second has been that commodifying parts does not mean commodifying the whole, either because people are not defined by their bodies ("I am my mind"), or because it is inappropriate to regard duplicate or renewable body parts as "integral" to a person.

I have some sympathy with the first point, which resonates with my own argument about monetary compensation for surrogacy not, of itself, transforming bodies into commodities or establishing a market. With bodily services, there is a hazy line between paying someone's expenses, compensating her for loss of earnings, expressing appreciation for her generosity, and buying her service, and while public policy tends to distinguish these according to the level of payment, it is not easy to separate them simply by the amount paid. The idea that a payment is "compensation," "appreciation," or "recompense"[18] if it clocks in under some (usually arbitrary) amount X, but becomes a "sale" when it reaches Y, is not entirely convincing. The difficulties in drawing the line have led some to conclude that no money should *ever* change hands. But the difficulties might equally well persuade us that paying "for" something is not enough to make it a commodity. As L. D. de Castro argues:

> We give monetary rewards to outstanding citizens for noteworthy accomplishments. We offer monetary incentives to

those who can contribute information leading to the arrest of criminals. We give monetary rewards to outstanding and dedicated teachers. We also give special monetary benefits to family members left behind by soldiers killed in battle. It does not usually cross our minds that the giving or acceptance of the reward may commodify the recipient or diminish the value of his or her contribution to society.[19]

On this account, it is a mistake to think that the mere exchange of money leads the person providing the body part, or the person receiving it, to regard the kidney (or egg or semen) as a tradable commodity. Payment need not mean something comes to bear a value characteriseable only in money terms. Additional motives and understandings are very often at work.

The literature on surrogacy provides evidence for this, for while most surrogates say they would not offer the service if there were *no* money involved, many also insist on their desire to help infertile or gay couples. There is some evidence of non-monetary motives in the market for semen, too, though here the fact that motives are sometimes nonmonetary does not always make them more attractive. In one study of sperm donors, Diane Tober identifies "a certain degree of egocentrism," and a desire on their part to spread around what they regard as their especially good genes.[20] So far as live kidney sales are concerned, however, there is virtually *no* evidence that those selling kidneys are also motivated by their desire to save a life. In a study of 305 kidney vendors in Chennai, India (conducted before the trade was officially banned), 96 percent of participants said they sold to pay off debts, and only 5 percent mentioned the wish to help a sick person with kidney disease as one among a number of factors.[21]

Had they stressed this more strongly as part of their motivation, we still could not regard this as settling the question. We cannot say there is no commodification going on so long as I (trying to decide whether to sell my kidney) am mildly interested in saving a life, and you (suffering from kidney damage) notice that I am a person as well as the source of a kidney. Defenders of the surrogacy contract sometimes make the point that the commissioning couple will be deeply aware of the surrogate as a person and very much concerned for her emotional and physical health.[22] Yet since it is virtually impossible not to notice that a person is a person, this cannot be taken as convincing evidence that they are not using her as a means to their end. Even in the most conventional of market arrangements, people remain people, and while the attitudes we adopt during a commercial transaction certainly matter to the quality of life, they do not of themselves change or determine what is taking place. However much time I spend chatting to the greengrocer, I am still expected to pay for my purchases. If I am sacked, it may slightly soften the blow if the person conveying the message views me as a long-standing colleague and friend, but I still lose my job.

Monetary and nonmonetary meanings do commonly coexist, and the fact that money changes hands does not determine that a transaction is primarily a monetary one. But the coexistence is much less marked in the sale of kidneys, and if this were the main defence against charges of commodification, it would be pretty unconvincing. On the whole, however, it is not a major plank in the case. For the most part, advocates of the market have been happy to acknowledge that the traded organ *is* being treated as a commodity and have focused attention on what they see as the mistaken conclusion that the person is therefore being treated as such. For Stephen Wilkinson

it's fairly easy to show why the objectification of persons might be thought wrong. Things are not so straightforward, however, when it comes down to bodies. And they are even less straightforward when it comes to bodily parts, products, and services. For, even if the objectification of persons is wrong, it doesn't follow from this (or at least, it doesn't follow obviously or directly) that there's something wrong with treating body parts as (mere) objects.[23]

Bodies, he continues, *are* objects, and are more than mere objects only "insofar as they are intimately related to persons."[24] The question then comes down to what it means to be intimately related. In the much-loved philosopher's example, we are asked to consider which is more "me": my brain, accidentally transplanted by some terrible medical confusion into someone else's body, or my body, now housing someone else's brain?[25] If forced to choose, I suspect many of us would opt for the unfamiliar body housing the familiar knowledges and memories— that would be my inclination, though if I rated my body more highly I can imagine making a different choice—but I do not think these fantastic scenarios do much to clarify the relationship people have to their bodies. Cécile Fabre remarks that we can get "a new heart, new lungs, new kidneys, new limbs, and new corneas, and remain the same person."[26] It is unlikely, however, that we could get a new skin colour or different sex without disruption to our sense of who we are, and hand and face transplants have proved notoriously traumatic because of the perception of hand and face as particularly intimate expressions of the person.[27] We do not just "have" our bodies. In an important sense, we "are" them.[28]

One might, of course, say the same about items we tend to regard as perfectly marketable. In an important sense, we might say, we "are" the books we read, the friends we make, the paintings we choose to put on our wall, so why pick out the body as peculiarly central to who we are? Are we so much more intimately bound up in our unchosen toes or kidneys than in the artefacts we have deliberately decided to surround ourselves with because of the ways they express our personality? Can we really defend the idea that our sense of self is so much more bound up in the parts of our body? These are good questions and are particularly pertinent given what I have argued about the difficulties of using "the body" to draw a firm line between activities that are legitimately marketable and those that are not. But claiming a similarity or continuum between bodies and not-bodies does not mean we stop worrying about what happens when body parts are treated as separable from the self. It might mean, to the contrary, that we should start worrying about what happens when we treat other things that way.

This, in essence, is what Margaret Radin argues.[29] In her critique of commodification, she makes little use of the "specialness" of the body, distinguishing, rather, between what she calls personal and fungible property. While bodies fall into the first camp (she is more willing than I to apply ownership terms to the body), there are many other things that should also be regarded as personal property, and *because of this*, not up for sale. Our identities are bound up with our bodies, but they can also, she argues, be intimately bound up with the house in which we have lived for years, or the ring given to us on our wedding day, and putting *any* of these on the market can cause extreme distress. (This provides us, among other things, with an argument for securing long-term tenancies.) In many ways, Radin plays down the significance of the body. In her argument, there are good reasons for keeping bodies out of the market, but these do not depend just on the fact of being a body, and arguments against markets in human organs need not depend on strong claims about what makes the body unique.

When Debra Satz explores why some things should be up for sale but not others, she too mostly discounts arguments about the specialness of the body, pointing out that our sense of identity might be more powerfully bound up in the book we are writing or the painting we have just completed than in our sexuality or capacity for becoming a mother.[30] The implication, for her, is that objections to markets in kidneys must be based on contingent, not essential, features. These markets are problematic, she argues, not because bits of the body are being sold, but because markets in body parts are characterised by weak agency, vulnerability, and inequality. They typically involve sellers who lack full information about the medical risks, who may, indeed, be deliberately deceived about these, and whose extreme poverty is the primary reason they sell. But it is these contingent features, Satz argues, not some magical character of bodies per se, that makes markets in human organs so problematic. In this argument, it is not the objectification or commodification that is the real problem, but the exploitative nature of the kidney market itself. Under radically different conditions, there might be no problem at all.

Contingent features of the existing markets are clearly a significant part of why people resist cash-for-kidneys, and the most plausible arguments for legalising organ sales have offered scenarios where these conditions are either subject to close regulation or imagined away. Fabre, for example, asks us to hypothesise a world in which everyone already has the right to the resources they need to live a minimally flourishing life, including access to a minimum income, housing, education, and basic health care, and only then to consider why those who want to "maximise their income by selling their organs" should not be permitted to do so.[31] In this scenario, the truly desperate exchange of the mother who sells her kidney in order to finance medical care for a dying child is simply eliminated from the picture. In related vein, Charles Erin and John Harris ask us to imagine a monopsonistic buyer like the UK's National Health Service as the only organisation licensed to purchase kidneys; to think of the kidneys being allocated to patients on the basis of medical need not purchasing power; and to envisage the purchasing zone being restricted to the recipients' region of the world, so as to reduce the chances of people in rich countries preying on those in poor.[32] With these conditions in place, they argue, there would no longer be such worries about the rich exploiting the poor and desperate, and the ethical objections would fall.

The Equality Objection

Arguments such as these operate at a high level of abstraction, either abstracting away the features that currently characterise markets in kidneys or skating over a host of practical problems. It would be extremely difficult, for example, to insulate the market in the way Erin and Harris suggest, and the risks of adding an underregulated legal market to the current illicit trade are too high to play around with.[33] Moreover, while their argument usefully disentangles concerns about commercialisation from concerns about inequality, it misses something crucial about the inequality implied in body part sales, something that—against Satz—I regard as a *non*contingent basis for objection. The point about body part sales is not just that people are driven to them by economic necessity, or that vendors are typically poor while purchasers are typically rich. Our entire world is premised on people doing things for money they would not do for love, and on richer people buying what poorer people sell. Markets thrive in conditions of inequality, and much of what they do is to bring together the money-poor with the money-rich. Insofar as they produce winners and losers, moreover, markets will generate and sustain all manner of further inequalities.

There is, nonetheless, a benign story that can be told about many markets as simply enabling specialisms: I am good at one thing, you are better at another, and if each of us concentrates our efforts on what we are better at and trade our respective products, we may both end up more prosperous. It is not, that is, *just* inequality that brings us to the market. We could start out with very much the same level of resources, and with roughly equal—but different—talents. Because those talents are different, however, it may still make sense to trade. Theorists of unequal exchange have pointed out the deceptions of this benign story of comparative advantage when it is produced to explain away inequities in international trade,[34] but there is still an intuitive truth to it. It is hard even to begin to tell that story about markets in body parts.

We all have bodies, and the universal availability of both product and capacities makes it implausible to imagine people as specialising in bodies per se. Variations in *kinds* of bodies clearly allow for specialisms—in athletic bodies or tall bodies or beautiful bodies—but billions of people the world over have a body, mostly including two working kidneys. In a world of social, economic, and gender equality, why would some of us choose, out of all possible activities, to specialise in kidney vending? It is hard to conceive what, in those circumstances, would propel anyone to sell, though it is correspondingly easy to imagine that many more people would offer to donate. If so, then the inequality that attends markets in body parts is not just a contingent but an intrinsic feature. There are no conceivable conditions under which the problem would disappear.

I noted earlier that the practice of commandeering the cadavers of executed criminals is now mostly considered indefensible, and I suggested that this reflected the increasing prevalence of ideas of equality that make it unacceptable to require of others what you would not do yourself. The idea that poverty or criminality disqualifies you from normal human consideration has not entirely disappeared (the lifetime disenfranchisement of convicted criminals in some parts of the United States remains a disturbing counterexample), but in general, we do not now divide humanity into different categories of being and attach different kinds of rights to each. In theory, at least, we recognise all as having the same basic rights. In doing so, we accept a commonsense version of the Kantian imperative to behave towards others as we would be willing for them to behave towards us.

The *donation* of human organs is entirely consistent with this. When grieving parents agree to the use of their child's organs, it is often with a sense that they do not want other parents to suffer the same kind of loss. When people sign up for postmortem donation, it may be because they know people who have received or are waiting for transplant organs and hope that their donation will help those in similar circumstances. Donors do not, on the whole, want compensation for organs, and this extends even to cases of live donation. Those offering themselves for a transplant operation may be willing to accept compensation for loss of wages or time off work but tend to say the act would be tainted if they accepted any more than that. Lewis Hyde cites an early study of (unpaid) kidney donors who went to considerable lengths to minimise the nature of the gift, so as to relieve the recipient of what otherwise could be an overwhelming burden of gratitude.[35] Recipients, meanwhile, may feel humbled by the generosity of the donors and may doubt whether they could have been so generous themselves. But they do not say donors *ought* to give in circumstances where they themselves would not dream of doing so, and they commonly express the hope that they would have been equally willing to donate had they been lucky enough to have two good kidneys. There is, in other words, a moral reciprocity in organ donation and an assumption that no more can be fairly asked of others than you would have been willing to do yourself. When organs are bought and sold, by contrast, the recipient benefits from an action he would never contemplate for himself (remember, he has to be relatively wealthy), and the fact of payment relieves him of any sense of reciprocal obligation.

Lawrence Cohen reports conversations with kidney recipients in India in which they explain their decision to buy rather than ask family members to donate in the following terms: "Why should I put a family member I care about at risk by asking him or her to donate an organ when I can just buy one?"[36] At one level, this sounds fair enough. We pay others to do many things we would not risk our own children doing, like fixing the roof and cutting down trees. We do not, however, normally frame this as a distinction between those we care about and those we do not: it is not that we do not care about the roofers' safety, or even, in this context, that we care more about our children's safety, but mostly that we think it better for the work to be done by trained professionals. Yet unlike markets in roofers and tree surgeons, the market in organs seems almost designed to ensure a division of the world into two kinds of being, with the fact of payment relieving the purchasers of any obligation to think themselves into the sellers' shoes. Donation encourages people to think more explicitly about their moral equality. It encourages the person with two good kidneys to think about what her life would have been like had she suffered kidney failure, and the person with kidney failure to think about what she would have been willing to do had she had two healthy kidneys. By contrast, market in kidneys encourages purchasers and sellers to think of themselves as beings apart. As Nancy Scheper-Hughes puts it, "kidney buyers engage in a kind of double-think, double-speak in which they discount living donations within the family, while recruiting organs from living strangers who are believed to 'benefit' enormously from the transaction."[37]

This is where the fact of us all having bodies is so pertinent, and where it being the *body* makes a difference. In the purchase of other kinds of service, we often feel we are buying something we would never ourselves sell. Perhaps we could not sell it, because we lack the necessary skills or training, but it may just be that we find the activity in some way unappealing. It is too risky, perhaps, or too tedious, or too much like hard work. Yet for some, even of these activities, it is reasonable to think that the person paid to carry them out views them in a different light: that the tree surgeon is less fearful of heights than I am and actively enjoys the challenge, that the postman likes getting up early and working out of doors, that the person doing routine office work enjoys bringing order out of chaos and appreciates not having to think about the work at the end of the day. It would be self-deceiving complacency to think this true of all jobs, to imagine there is someone out there suited to every unpleasant task, or that those doing jobs I would hate are different enough in their tastes to be perfectly happy in their work. But the variety of tastes and aptitudes is still significant enough for us to be able to imagine a world organised in such a way as to minimise the number doing work they actively dislike.

I am reminded here of Charles Fourier—one of those Marx described as a utopian socialist—who sought to reconcile the necessity for work with the desire for happiness by organising communities that contained within them the full range of human types (he thought 1,620 the optimum number). By matching tasks to type and arranging things so that everyone carried out a variety of tasks each day, he believed we could ensure that none of us was engaged in labour we disliked.[38] Fourier's dream of eliminating all unpleasant work is pretty utopian. But it is not entirely delusional to note that different kinds of people enjoy different kinds of work, or to think that specialisation can be made compatible with equality. One might, indeed, envisage it as the goal of social change that no one should be required to do work they hate; if some tasks are so loathsome that no one would willingly choose them, they should be either eliminated by technological innovation or else shared out. Rajeev Bhargava discusses the Bhangis of India's caste system who are assigned by birth to the work of removing human waste, including from dry toilets and open-gutter latrines.[39] The colonial administrators adopted the romantic designation of "night soil" to describe this work, but as Bhargava stresses, the work is physically repugnant—the body revolts from it—and its irreducible materiality demeans people in their own eyes as well as those of others. If we are to deliver on the promise of human equality, this looks to be one form of work that simply has to be abolished. "No matter how hard one tries to alter its social meanings or change the nature of its surrounding conditions, and no matter how voluntary it becomes, when it is performed persistently over a period of time it alters one's self-esteem and the attitude of others in such a way that it is bound to be degrading."[40]

I introduce this example, not because I see selling one's kidney as a physically repugnant activity, but to illustrate my general claim that some divisions of labour are incompatible with equality: not just "normally accompanied" by inequality, but inseparable from it. It is not, to repeat, delusional to think that a social division of labour can be made compatible with equality.

It is, I believe, delusional to think that specialising in organ vending can be made compatible in this way.

Markets in human organs rely on a systemic inequality between recipients and vendors that has the effect of denying our moral equality. The fact that it is the body that is up for sale matters, not because our identities are intimately bound up with all the parts of our bodies, but because we all have bodies. If some of us nonetheless become positioned as sellers and others as buyers, the only conceivable explanation lies in our inequality. We may appeal to differences in taste and talent to explain and justify other kinds of specialisation, and while the explanation will often be meretricious (the real reason you clean my house while I write my book is not that you love cleaning, but that I got lucky in my access to education), it remains available as a possible reason. It is not inconceivable that this is the explanation; it is just likely that there are other factors at work, either instead or as well. In the decision to become a vendor rather than purchaser of organs, by contrast, neither taste nor talent can conceivably be involved. Inequality is the only explanation.

My own favoured solution for addressing the shortage of transplant organs is a well-advertised and regulated system of presumed consent, with people actively opting out of becoming organ donors rather than, as is the practice in many countries, opting in. I do not mean, by this, the kind of presumed consent that operates in some parts of the United States, where it comes into play on the occasion of a mandatory autopsy, and therefore applies disproportionately to murder victims, who in turn are disproportionately African American and/or poor.[41] The legitimacy of presumed consent requires that it applies to all; that there are easily accessed ways of opting out; and that its provisions are well advertised across society, with particular attention paid to those from minority language groups, such that people are aware that the system operates. We should have the fullest possible opportunity to withdraw from the scheme, but the default position would be that everyone's organs become available, where suitable, for transplant and research.

It is notable that advocates of a market often also support presumed consent, but since they anticipate that any resulting increase in donation will still be inadequate to the demand, argue that this should be supplemented by monetary incentives to live donors. From a property perspective, this combination of proposals is pretty strange. In its own mild way, presumed consent queries the scope and dominance of private property (this is one reason it remains controversial) while payment to live donors seems to instantiate private property rights in the body. Under a system of presumed consent, I think of my body as a resource that becomes available for others when it is no longer of use to me and do not anticipate charging those others for the privilege. My relationship to my body then becomes closer to the relationship to the land under systems of communal land tenure: the body is very much mine so long as I use it, but is not mine to sell. I owe it, in some sense, to others when I can no longer use it.[42] The two proposals then make for an awkward combination. It seems odd to set up a system that encourages people to sell their organs when alive, but expects them, failing any conscientious objection, to give them away on death.

In Fabre's account, the argument becomes odder still, for her main concern is not with the permissibility of organ sales, but with establishing that "the sick have a right, as a matter of justice, to (some of) the body parts of healthy adults."[43] If those worse off have a moral right to the material resources they need to lead a minimally flourishing life, then those lacking vital body parts have a similar moral right to the spare body parts of those more favoured. Having argued that it is legitimate to confiscate live body parts from the healthy in order to save or ameliorate the lives of the sick, it may seem odd that Fabre even bothers with the legitimacy of markets. If the basic need is met by confiscation, why also argue for the right to sell? She anticipates the need for markets arising only in relatively limited circumstances: where the sick have in some way relinquished their entitlement to new organs, perhaps by knowingly doing something that endangered their health; or the relatively healthy want more or better organs (the athlete who can function with one kidney but will manage better with two); or where the potential vendor sees this as a way to raise money for his own basic projects. It is not that society might require this additional source of organs in order to meet pressing medical need, but more that people should have this right. Interestingly, the argument does not rest directly on property claims. The point is not that this is *my* body, to dispose of as *I* choose. To the contrary, Fabre seeks to convince us that others have a legitimate claim on some of what we might have regarded as our exclusive possession, and she frames the additional right to buy and sell as an autonomy rather than property right, as the right to frame, revise, and implement our conceptions of the good. The crucial move in her argument is not about bodies being property (property does not figure in the index of the book), but bodies being material resources. It matters to the argument that bodies are not special, but the argument is not grounded in a property claim.

Property as Protection: Using Property against Property?

This relative indifference to property claims goes beyond the specificities of Fabre's argument. John Harris works within a very different philosophical framework, favouring the language of costs and benefits over the language of rights, but then, even more definitively than Fabre, is not in the business of shoring up property rights. In general, there has been relatively little emphasis on self-ownership or the property we have in our bodies among advocates of the market, and often a strong attachment to property rights among those resisting commodification. I began this chapter with the work of Andrews and Nelkin, who see the explosion of interest in body parts and tissues as bringing about a highly disturbing fragmentation and commodification. This is a problem, in their view, because it decontextualises the body, reducing to the status of mere utilitarian object what is better understood as a "social, ritual and metaphorical entity, and *the only thing many people can really call their own*"[44] (my italics). As the comment suggests, their solution lies, not in a refusal of body property, but in a stronger affirmation of ownership rights. We need enhanced knowledge and control over what is being done with our body parts and tissues, rigorous enforcement of our rights to informed consent, and legal recognition of the body as property. In this argument, "our" property rights can work to block "their" property claims. "Courts and other policymakers should make clear that, even if an individual can treat his or her body as property, others should not be able to do so."[45] Asserting the individual's body rights becomes the most effective way to protect the body from the market.

I return, then, to a tension set out in early chapters. Because property language has often been the medium through which we claim personal rights, a way to claim control over our lives and resist the intrusions of others, it has figured as both support to commodification and opponent. As regards the sale of intimate bodily services, it most plausibly figures as support, for even if the language of renting or property is not widely used, ownership of the body provides one basis for the right to engage in such sales and the enforceability of the associated contracts. As regards markets in body tissues and parts, it figures as both, but it sometimes seems to be those most concerned to regulate and limit the trade who invoke property on their side. In particular, the idea that we need property rights to contest the power of global companies, gain redress from the misdirection of donated organs, or secure control over the "downstream" uses of our body parts, is widely canvassed. I have noted that Donna Dickenson sees property in the person—though not, in her analysis, property in the body—as a crucial protection for women against the abuses of their reproductive labour.[46] Many go further, to represent property in the body as the crucial resource. From the *Moore* judgment onwards—described by one critic as "outrageous"[47]—it has been argued that the refusal of courts to acknowledge people as having a property in their bodies serves the interests of research institutions and biotechnology companies while leaving individuals with no compensation or return.[48] In Nils Hoppe's analysis, "the spectre of exploitability leads the law to prohibit profiteering *using our own bodies* but at the same time licenses legal and illegal profiteering of *other individuals' bodies.*"[49] On this argument, those who see it as ethically unsavoury to think of people as owning their bodies are licensing the pharmaceutical and biotechnological companies to get away with rhetorical murder.

The profits that can be made from people's bodies are extraordinary, and the discrepancy between what research companies or hospitals can make and what "donors" or "sources" get can be extreme. The researchers who took John Moore's body tissues and created from them (without his knowledge or consent) the lucrative "Mo cell-line" benefitted substantially from the patent taken out on their research, as did the University of California. On some estimates, that patent could be worth

$3 billion. John Moore got nothing. The researchers who took Henrietta Lacks's tumorous cells (again, without her knowledge or consent) to produce "HeLa," the first human cell line grown in laboratory conditions, did not, in fact, benefit financially.[50] But with more than 50 million tonnes of HeLa since grown for medical research, many other people did. Henrietta Lacks got nothing and was buried in an unmarked grave. In a particularly unhappy coda to her story, her surviving children cannot afford the health insurance that would enable them to buy the drugs made possible by their mother's cells.

At a less astronomical level, relatives approving the donation of a body within a marketised health system, such as operates in the United States, may be contributing significantly to the profits of the hospital, for recipients of transplant organs are charged not only the cost of the operation but a price—which can reach many thousands of dollars—for the organ itself. Again, we hear of cases in which the donor's family could not even afford to erect a headstone for the person who died.[51] Problems also arise when donations are made to explicitly non-profit-making bodies like tissue banks, because (in the United States, at least) many of these are partnered with private companies, and the downstream uses of the profits can generate large profits. Suzanne Holland estimates that the typical altruistic donation could later yield up to $34,000 in downstream sales, and that one "high-quality" cadaver could be worth as much as $220,000.[52]

Cases like Moore and Lacks offend many people's sense of fairness, though not necessarily to the point of saying that the donor or donor's family should receive a percentage of the profits. Courts and companies have, somewhat predictably, been opposed to profit sharing, mostly on the grounds that it would inhibit research. This is a dubious argument: if research is inhibited by the requirement to pay for components, that would also be an argument against paying universities for the use of their research facilities, or paying researchers for their time. The more compelling objection is the randomness of whose cells turn out to have uniquely useful qualities, like the capacity for dividing and reproducing outside the body. The unfairness in the current dispensation is not that John Moore or Henrietta Lacks got no more from the use of their valuable body tissues than did Fred Smith or Suzy Parker from their valueless ones, for the chance differences that make some tissues medically valuable and others not are very much the luck of the draw and would hardly justify Moore and Lacks becoming millionaires while Smith and Parker remain in poverty. There is an unfairness, but it lies in the fact that resources that could not have come into being without the contribution of patients end up entirely at the disposal of profit-making companies. There is a strong case for a levy on the proceeds of this kind of research, to be returned, either as assistance to the specific group suffering from the disease, or to the wider community. Known in the field as "benefit sharing," this could take the form of requiring companies to provide technology transfer or to contribute to the development of health care facilities. The Human Genome Organisation has recommended an annual levy of up to 3 percent of net profits of profit-making bodies that rely on human tissue be distributed in this way.[53]

Those arguing for a clearer recognition of property rights in the body do not, on the whole, think Moore should have benefitted personally from the profits, or that relatives of organ donors should get payment per organ. Some argue for benefit sharing, but most have been less preoccupied with what happens to the money and more with patient control. Under current conditions, for example, donors may be unaware that some of what they are donating will be used for cosmetic rather than therapeutic purposes. Suzanne Holland gives the example of a couple who approved the donation of their daughter's skin tissue to a non-profit-making tissue bank, only to discover that it had been sold on to a company dealing in cosmetic enhancement.[54] Donors may also give their consent for tissues to be stored by particular researchers for particular research purposes, only later to discover that the tissue bank has been transferred to other hands.

In the case of *The Washington University v. Dr. W. Catalona et al.*, a prostate cancer specialist employed by Washington University had built up a substantial tissue repository to assist his research and sought to take it with him when he later moved to Northwestern University.[55] Despite getting the support of six thousand former patients, all agreeing they had meant their tissue for the use of Dr. Catalona, the court decided in favour of the property claims of Washington University. The judge argued, among other things, that allowing donors to choose who could keep their samples was like allowing blood donors to restrict the use of their blood to specific ethnic groups.[56] In *Greenberg v. Miami Children's Hospital*, Dan and Debbie Greenberg, whose son suffered from the fatal Canavan disease, had taken the initiative in securing body tissue and genetic material from a worldwide network of sufferers, and this enabled a medical researcher to isolate the relevant gene.[57] When the researcher moved, however, to the Miami Children's Hospital, his new employer filed for a patent for the genetic sequence, with a view, partly, to the royalty fees it could charge future sufferers for using it in diagnostic treatment. In this case, the court upheld a claim of "unjust enrichment" against the hospital, but was still at pains to affirm that there can be no property in the body.

Some have argued that in the absence of clearly recognised property rights, there is also insufficient redress if body tissues are stolen, organs donated for one purpose end up being used for another, or body samples being stored for patients are later lost. There was a period in the 1990s at the Center for Reproductive Health of the University of California when eggs and embryos from one patient were being routinely implanted in another, without either's knowledge or consent. One way of describing this would be to say that the eggs and embryos were stolen, but because they could not be legally recognised as property, there was said to be no basis for extraditing the doctor responsible when he later fled across the border to Mexico. As Andrews and Nelkin caustically observe: "the body is not a legally recognized 'property' under the law, so biocrime is not a legally recognized offense."[58] In the English case of *Regina v. Kelly*, also from the 1990s, an artist and laboratory technician who had been convicted of stealing anatomical specimens from the Royal College of Surgeons tried to turn the notion about bodies not being property to use in their defence.[59] They appealed against conviction on the grounds that body parts belong to no one; hence, there could be no theft. The judges agreed that neither a corpse nor part of one is capable of being property, but in a classically Lockean application, argued that the work subsequently carried out on the specimens—dissection, preservation, and so on— was enough to make them the property of the college. In the case of the eggs and embryos, there was apparently no theft. In the case of the anatomical specimens, there was, but only because of a somewhat convoluted argument about mixing one's labour with a body part. A more straightforward recognition of property in bodies might secure more immediate redress.

It might also, it is argued, provide a better basis for dealing with medical negligence. In *Colavito v. New York Organ Donor Network*, a woman had donated her deceased husband's kidneys to a family friend. One of the two kidneys was allocated to another patient, and only then did the surgeons discover that the one intended for Colavito was irreparably damaged. He claimed compensation on the basis of a property right, but lost on the usual "no property in the body" grounds.[60] In *Yearworth & others v. North Bristol NHS Trust*, the claimants had been encouraged to store semen samples before undergoing chemotherapy and later submitted a claim for damages when errors in the storage process meant the semen was irretrievably damaged.[61] Their claim, too, was refused on classic "no property in the body" grounds. In this case, however, the judgment was later modified on appeal. Carefully reviewing the legal precedents on body property, the appeal court recognised in the men "a fundamental right of ownership" as evidenced in their absolute right to determine when or if their sperm was destroyed. Nils Hoppe cites this departure from previous judgments as an "excellent and lucid" judgment.[62]

Significantly for those who look to property as strengthening personal control, the judgment drew on Anthony Honoré's account of ownership as involving a number of distinct and separable rights, not necessarily including the absolute right to sell. Recall that in debates about whether we can be said to own ourselves, political theorists have tended to assume that self-ownership means absolute rights of alienation and control. In G. A. Cohen's definition, "to own oneself is to enjoy with respect to oneself all those rights which a slaveowner has over a complete chattel slave."[63] In Honoré's account, by contrast, owning something can mean a range of things, not all of which will be found together. Ownership might mean the right to sell, or to the income that can be derived from your property, but might also—or instead—mean the right to remain in physical possession, the right to use the property, to determine how others use it, and so on.[64] Even where private property holds sway, the rights of property owners are rarely untrammelled (in most jurisdictions, landlords cannot simply evict long-term tenants from "their" property without going through some kind of legal process), while under collective or communal ownership, there may be very limited rights to sell. Much of the land in precolonial West Africa, for example, was held under systems of communal property. Individuals had secure rights to farm "their" land, including the right to pass it on to their children, but the land was regarded as belonging ultimately to the community and could not be sold to strangers without that community's consent. (Since the chiefs had the ultimate authority to decide this on the community's behalf, many of them got very rich.[65]) Honoré's account of ownership provides a better basis for recognising the range and variety of rights attached to property and helps steer us away from the absolutist accounts expressed in images of the slave owner and chattel slave. The *Yearworth* judges cite him approvingly as showing that ownership is "a convenient global description of different collections of rights held by persons over physical and other things,"[66] and were thereby enabled to recognise *one* right of property—the "right to use at one's discretion"—without committing themselves on whether the men enjoyed all the others.

This, broadly, has been the favoured strategy of those who invoke property rights as a way to secure ourselves against the commodification and exploitation of the body. Honoré's account is widely cited.[67] Property, we are told, is neither unified nor absolute. It is better understood as a "bundle of sticks," some of which must be present before we can reasonably talk of property, but rarely, if ever, all. Claiming some property rights can then be a way of preventing others. It is not, in this account, property claims that encourage commodification, but their relative absence.

What is wrong with this? There is a practical objection, outlined in chapter one, to the effect we cannot simply make property mean what we want it to mean. The notion of property rights as endowing the possessor with absolute power may be theoretically discredited and at odds with the more complex and nuanced ways in which property is understood in legal discourse and practice. But so long as the more absolutist understanding continues to hold sway over popular imagination, claims to property in the body will be widely understood as legitimating the sale of bodily services and parts rather than resisting this development. What Richard Gold calls "the blinders of contemporary property discourse"[68] encourage us to consider things claimed as property, first, as our own (so subject to our own choices and decisions, not to be determined or limited by others), and second, as appropriately traded in a market. On Honoré's or Dickenson's account, this is only one possible meaning. But in the translation from theoretical to practical discourse, concepts tend to resume the shape they had before their theoretical refinement, and we cannot just make them mean what we want them to mean.[69]

The practical objection is even stronger when those putting the "progressive" case for property are explicitly recommending redefinition. When Rosalind Petchesky, for example, made her case for women to claim their bodies as property, she recognised that what she had in mind was a different understanding of property, one less indebted to abstract individualism or mind/body dualism and more informed by notions of caretaking, nurturance, and collective—rather than private—authority over resources.[70] But why would this alternative understanding of property take root? Jennifer Nedelsky observes that "an extraordinary range of theorists have recognized the power of property in our political and legal discourse and have proposed redefining it as a vehicle for change." In her view (and mine), "such proposals consistently underestimate the power of the traditional conceptions of property and the inequality that goes with them."[71]

Underlying this is a deeper objection, which is that looking to property as protection still leaves us with individuals determining what can or can't be done. Consider again the argument in *Washington University v. Dr. W. Catalona et al.*, to the effect that allowing donors to choose which researchers have access to their samples is like allowing blood donors to specify that their blood can only be used for members of particular ethnic groups. The analogy is not, to my mind, compelling, because the first issue has large financial implications, while the second should be a matter of medical need. But putting the two together does raise questions. It seems reasonable to say—with Suzanne Holland—that someone donating material for research into life-saving therapies should have the right to insist that it is not used for commercial or cosmetic purposes. But it also seems plausible to say—with John Harris—that those donating material for research purposes should not have the right to determine which illnesses are to be the research priority or which groups of patients are to benefit from the research. Do we think sperm donors should have the right to restrict the use of their sperm to heterosexual women, or egg donors the use of their eggs to those who share their religion? And if not, why not? If the right to determine that our material not be used for commercial purposes we disapprove of arises out of ownership rights, why wouldn't we have exactly the same right to refuse permission for these other purposes? Why would we be allowed to dictate in some cases but not others?

The answer lies, not in some mysterious quality of property, but in the social judgment that health differs from cosmetics, a judgment validated in public discussion and usually enshrined in the funding practices for health care provision. The important point is that it is social. Societies decide, ideally though not usually, through processes of inclusive political deliberation, to allow citizens some rights but not others. We are authorised to make certain kinds of decisions for ourselves, but not others; thus, we can choose whether or not to donate blood, but not whether to serve on a jury, or we can decide for ourselves whether to undergo what the doctors tell us is a life-saving operation, but cannot require them to perform an operation they believe would be useless. If the right to control downstream uses of donated tissues and parts were grounded in property, it would be hard to explain why the person who disapproves of gays should not have exactly the same rights of control as the person who disapproves of cosmetic surgery. If we want to differentiate, it must be on other grounds.

Property per se does little to help us in addressing the dilemmas thrown up by new developments in medical and reproductive technology. Property claims focus our attention too narrowly on the individual and his or her rights. Yet the dilemmas involve the kind of society we want to live in, including whether it will be one that delivers on the promise of treating all as equals. There is a serious mismatch here, and it is to this that I turn in the final chapter.

CHAPTER FIVE

The Individualism
of Property Claims

The first man who, having enclosed a piece of ground, be-
thought himself of saying "This is mine," and found people
simple enough to believe him, was the real founder of civil
society. From how many crimes, wars, and murders, from
how many horrors and misfortunes might not any one have
saved mankind, by pulling up the stakes, or filling up the
ditch, and crying to his fellows: "Beware of listening to this
imposter; you are undone if you once forget that the fruits
of the earth belong to us all, and the earth itself to nobody."[1]

IN ROUSSEAU'S CRITIQUE of property in land, he offers us
three scenarios. Something belongs to all, it belongs to nobody, and/or people who have no more right to it than anyone
else illegitimately claim it as their own. At first sight, none of
the options works especially well with bodies. But the imposter
laying claim to something that arguably belongs to all makes
his reappearance in the shape of universities and biotechnology companies turning materials donated for general benefit
to their own private profit. Despite disturbing connotations,
something akin to the idea of bodies belonging to all also figures in contemporary arguments that represent human gametes
as a shared resource,[2] or favour benefit sharing for the resources

generated with tissues excised from bodies during operations, or argue for a system of presumed consent to the postmortem use of bodies. As regards the last, I have indicated my sympathy for an understanding of the deceased body as in some sense part of the commons, but do not take my stand on a communism of the body. My arguments drive more in the direction of bodies belonging to nobody. More precisely—because "belonging to" is not the same as "being owned by"—I have sought in this book to challenge the idea that bodies can be understood as property.

It is not that our bodies do not "belong" to us; they certainly belong to us rather than to our spouses or employers or neighbours. But just as we can say we belong to a club without seeing ourselves as either owning or being owned by it, so we can say our bodies belong to us without claiming ownership over them. It is important, moreover, not to take that further step, and this becomes especially apparent when we turn to the policy implications that might flow from notions of the body as property. Despite all we now know about property as a social construction, framing bodily rights in terms of property still drags us back to ideas of something vested in us before society took hold, rights we have independently of what society permits us, rights we have just because something is ours. This remains the dominant understanding even when actual property rights are self-evidently dependent on the social and legal institutions that craft and sustain them. We can all, for sure, see that property rights are both circumscribed and secured by law, that they change through time, and that they vary from one society to another. But saying "circumscribed" still gives it away, suggesting something previously more powerful that has been reduced, cut down, curtailed, by political intervention or bureaucratic regulation. Even when we recognise its historical variability, the language of property encourages us to conceive of its rights and claims as grounded in something prior to or independent of social convention. If we consistently thought of our property rights as contingent and socially constructed, we could not attach the same note of indignation to claims about their violation.

I have no objection to rights that transcend particular societies. I am perfectly happy to have my rights enshrined in transnational conventions and to talk the language of human rights. Whilst it is evident, moreover, that rights have a history—that people did not always claim rights in the name of humanity, and did not always claim such rights as bodily integrity—I do not take this to mean they only now exist in societies that have decided to attach weight to them. My questions are, what is added by framing bodily rights as property rights, and what is lost when we do so? I suggested earlier that more general notions of human right or need encourage practices of reciprocity that engage with the significance we should attach to all persons, while the claims of property are burdened by their associations with inequality. I return to this theme now, focusing on consequences as regards public policy. I do not set out detailed policy recommendations for all the currently controversial areas: what regulations, if any, to propose for prostitution, surrogacy, the marketing of human gametes, the patenting of human DNA, the storage of human bodily tissues, the marketing of live human organs, and so on. There are general guidelines that follow relatively clearly from my arguments, and some particularly difficult questions that I address directly in this chapter. But policy always has to be made with an eye to what currently exists within a given society—what rules are currently in force, what kinds of practices and norms, what possibilities these open up, what obstacles they place in the way—and it is not, on the whole, useful to draw up detailed recommendations regardless of context. I do, however, want to lay out one general argument about the way property paradigms constrain the making of social policy and follow up with a more elaborated discussion of two particularly challenging policy concerns.

Property Paradigms and the Constraints on Policy

Property paradigms constrain the making of policy by restricting the range of relevant considerations and making the individual the centre of concern. There is a pervasive individualism in pretty much all rights claims (even seemingly group rights to cultural heritage or national self-determination can be redescribed in terms of the individual), but the individual comes especially powerfully to the fore in the world of property rights. When we assert ownership over something, we assert our interests and preferences as the predominant concern, as the interests and preferences that are rightfully protected against marauding strangers and the incursions of the state. Although that assertion of ownership does not occlude other interests or preferences—ownership rights, recall, are not absolute—it significantly narrows the range of issues that will be brought to bear in formulating public policy. It means we take what works for those individual owners as the starting point for our deliberations. This makes it harder to address consequences at the level of society as a whole.

Consider again the arguments in favour of markets in bodily materials and services. Where markets in bodily services are concerned, explicit parallels with property are muted, and it is relatively rare to hear the language of renting out applied to the body. Where markets in body parts are concerned, the central argument in favour is often a society-level one: that more people will live more flourishing lives as a result. In both cases, however, there is a crucial line of argument that refers to the rights people have to do as they choose with their bodies, and the satisfactions they derive as individuals from making these choices. Property links to choice and choice becomes justification. It is, of course, recognised, even by the keenest advocate of body markets, that the circumstances in which individuals make their choices are far from ideal. When we consider what prompts people to choose sex work as their favoured activity, or to offer a kidney for sale, it is evident that they are choosing from a limited set of alternatives. But why, we are asked, further curtail that limited set? We might think, with Richard Titmuss, that relying on money exchanges to secure supplies of blood damages the moral fabric of society, leading to an erosion of altruistic motives. We might think, with the Nuffield Council on Bioethics, that there is a "common good of altruistic donation," and that governments have a responsibility to do what they can to sustain this.[3] But why should the rights of the more vulnerable be denied so that the rest of us can enjoy our higher moral ground? Why should they be expected to pay the price for maintaining this better society?

That restricting markets further reduces the options for those who already have little choice is a serious charge, and I return to this below as one of the challenges to my position. The point I want to stress here is that in devising social policy, we need to address a range of considerations, including the rights of individuals, the welfare of individuals, the consistency of a proposed policy with other principles and policies, its chances of success, and the likely consequences of its implementation at the level of society as whole. One of the problems with the language of property is that it preempts that wider range of considerations with simpler assertions about the property being mine. "It's my body and I can do what I like with it" is the perennial cry. Through that property claim, we are warned that the only challenges we can legitimately make are either proving to you that what you like to do is interfering with my rights or proving that it isn't *really* what you like. If I prefer not to question either your agency or your judgment (and as I have indicated in my discussion of surrogacy, I prefer to steer clear of that ground), and have no compelling evidence that you are damaging me, then I have reached the limits of reasonable objection. Claiming something as a property right locates its significance firmly within the individual, and while I can suggest to you that your choices might have unfortunate consequences for society as whole, it remains up to you whether to take this into account. The focus, to adopt terminology from Debra Satz, is almost exclusively on the microlevel. Macrolevel considerations only register to the extent that you decide to accept them.

Yet it is at this macrolevel that some of the most compelling issues arise: is it the case that body markets drive out altruistic motives, weaken bonds of reciprocity, or make us less capable of viewing others as our equals? In her analysis of prostitution and surrogacy, Satz rigorously avoids recourse to the "specialness" of the body. She also avoids, or at least leaves unresolved, empirical claims about the damage people can do to their self-esteem or the risks of self-alienation. Since the relationship people have to their sexuality is diverse, we cannot presume that prostitution is more harmful to the individual than other commercial transactions; since the ways in which women experience pregnancy are diverse, we cannot presume that contract pregnancy is experienced as self-alienation. Instead of engaging in claims and counterclaims about what the average or "normal" woman feels, Satz encourages us to consider the effects at the level of society as a whole. Prostitution, she argues, "is a theatre of inequality; it displays for us a practice in which women are seen as servants of men's desires."[4] This remains the case even if specific clients do not see it this way and specific prostitutes do not experience it as such. It is because of the *asymmetry*, the way it contributes to women's inferior social status, that the practice is so problematic. Her parallel argument regarding surrogacy is that in giving others increased control over women's bodies and reinforcing views of women as baby machines, it "reinforces a long history of group-based inequality."[5] Again, it is the asymmetry that is at issue: "current gender inequality lies at the heart of what is wrong with pregnancy contracts."[6]

The point about this kind of argument—as about my own argument in chapter four about body markets promoting ideas of human *in*equality—is that it cannot even take hold unless we are willing to go beyond the experiences of those most directly involved. If analysis of prostitution or surrogacy, for example, rests only on how the participants experience it, we may uncover damning evidence for some sectors of the trade (street prostitutes, perhaps, or surrogates in surrogacy hostels), but we will surely discover that not everyone finds the work either harmful or destructive. In chapter three I expressed some scepticism about the self-descriptions and argued that the absence of overt or self-declared damage can also be taken as evidence of the hard work surrogates have had to do in managing their emotions. But even allowing for this, it is clear that many—including those working in the commercial sector—express satisfaction in their work. As regards markets in body parts, it is entirely implausible to claim some basis in comparative advantage that pleasantly divides the world into buyers and sellers, but it is not so entirely implausible to think of surrogacy, at least, in this way. Some women get more satisfaction out of being pregnant than others, some find it easier than others to be pregnant without feeling they are forming a relationship with a child, and if we do vary in this way, why assume that surrogacy is damaging to all? On this account, we should perhaps focus policy on establishing rigorous precontract counselling services to detect those women who can best sustain an emotional separation between pregnancy and motherhood and screen out the rest. In her discussion of the Baby M case, Rosemarie Tong suggests that the surrogacy agency rushed prematurely into matching Mary Beth Whitehead with the Sterns because of a striking physical resemblance between Whitehead and Elizabeth Stern and did not sufficiently investigate whether Whitehead had the emotional capacity to relinquish a child. Let us agree that some women are better at relinquishing than others, perhaps because they have completed their own families, or because they have never wanted children of their own, or just because of something in their personality. If we can organise the trade to identify these individuals, no one is going to be harmed.

In debates about prostitution, we also hear this kind of argument. Claims about it being degrading or alienating for a woman to provide bodily intimacy to a paying stranger are countered by claims about sex workers developing the capacity to detach themselves from what they are doing with their bodies, and even claims about them actively enjoying it. Some of this is just reassuring fantasy, but it is apparent, from everyday attitudes to casual sex, that people vary. Some find it relatively easy to separate sexual encounter from emotional attachment; some find it hard to experience sexual attraction in the context of a close attachment; others find it difficult to experience sexual attraction except in the context of that close attachment. So maybe the problem with prostitution, too, is only that some of those doing the job are poorly matched to it: that too many sex workers have been drawn from the ranks of those who find sex with unknown and (to them) unattractive strangers degrading. If the matching were done better, and only those with well-developed distancing mechanisms took up the profession, all would be well.

In the case of prostitution, this sounds and is entirely implausible. We know perfectly well there is no way of ensuring this kind of match; that a significant proportion of sex workers remain in their work because of drug addiction; and that even the more regulated systems, in countries where prostitution is legal, do not engage in anything like a counselling service before signing people on to the job. But note, also, that any such arguments depend exclusively on how the individuals involved experience sex work or surrogacy. They do not engage with the wider questions Satz and others want us to address as regards consequences for society as a whole. The individualism inherent in property claims makes it difficult to engage with macro-level concerns. And this is not just accident. Advocates of the property paradigm are fully aware of this restriction and often explicitly endorse it. They do not accept that individuals should be constrained in their choices by anything other than the direct harm their actions could bring about. They do not accept nebulous claims about actions corroding altruism or promoting practices of inequality, both because of (real) difficulties in establishing causal connections and because this is not, in their view, the responsibility of the individuals concerned.

In my arguments so far, I have stressed that thinking of oneself as in a relationship of ownership to one's body does *not* commit one, in some inevitable chain of consequences, to supporting the commodification of the body and promoting markets in bodily services and parts. What it does do, however, is skew the kinds of argument that become available when societies are considering policies on body matters. Property claims make the individual property owners the centre of attention and establish their preferences and choices as the predominant concerns. As Heather Widdows puts it, the emphasis on the choices of the individuals most directly concerned "effectively privatises,"[7] pushing out what are then perceived as abuses of governmental authority to promote nebulous notions of the common good. The individualism of property language and property rights drives out macrolevel considerations. It makes it harder for societies to address society-level effects, and casts a pall of suspicion over objectives like "promoting solidarity," "maintaining reciprocity," or "encouraging altruistic practices." Those most committed to the individualism of property claims will recoil in horror from the suggestion that governments should be engaged in any such social engineering. Others are more likely to recoil in horror from the idea that all this should be left to the intended and unintended consequences of individual choice. I put myself in the second camp.

Policies (a): Banning Markets

So what, in more detail, of specific policies? One of the objections to the kind of arguments I have developed is that if they imply a summary ban on body commodification, this makes the most vulnerable even worse off. As Janet Radcliffe Richards puts it, "If our ground for concern is that the range of choices is too small, we cannot improve matters by removing the best option that poverty has left, and make the range smaller still."[8] Even Margaret Radin warns that justice may not be best served by banning sales of human organs or sexual services, since for those with few alternatives, selling what little they have may be the only way to a humane existence. If society is not otherwise proposing to ameliorate poverty and expand people's choice sets, how can we justify taking away one of their few remaining choices?

The simple, if somewhat weaselly, answer is that I do not think all bodily trades should be summarily banned. I could not coherently argue this even if it were my preferred position, given what I have suggested about the problems in using "the body" to draw a definitive line. I believe, moreover, that policies must be devised with a view to unintended as well as intended effects, and that this can mean tolerating, even endorsing, practices one otherwise condemns. I might condemn child labour, for example, but also believe that an outright ban makes both children and their families much worse off. Instead of campaigning for immediate prohibition, I might then work for transitional arrangements that bridge the income gap. Or I might be critical of religiously based education and think children should be educated together in nondenominational schools. If, however, it is established practice in a country for the state to fund large numbers of schools for those of the majority religion, I might argue, on equity grounds, that it should fund additional schools for those from minority religions. In the first case, I would be arguing that a practice I condemn should nonetheless persist, for at least a while longer. In the second case, I would be actively promoting its extension. Policy recommendations do not flow neatly from philosophical premises, precisely because they have to take account of a range of considerations.

Where markets are already thoroughly embedded, as is the case with prostitution, I do not favour prohibitions that criminalise sex workers or make their working conditions more dangerous, and I think policies should be tailored with a view to the welfare of sex workers as well as effects on general practices of gender equality. Where there are options that enable a non-commercial version of a bodily service, as is the case with surrogacy, I favour that. But where markets in human organs are concerned, the issue is not whether to ban existing legal trade, but whether to lift bans that are already widely in place. In the light of what I have argued about markets in live human organs depending on circumstances of severe material inequality, and producing and reproducing social practices of inequality, I see no case for this. It is a counsel of despair to say that governments must never pass legislation that restricts options for the most vulnerable. On that basis, there could never be legislation setting minimum wage levels, banning child labour, or requiring employers to provide equal pay for women and men. In desperate situations, there will always be individuals prepared to work for rewards and in conditions that their fellow workers have deemed unacceptable. This is part of why legislation matters.

When a government sets maximum working hours or minimum holiday entitlements or introduces parental leave, it becomes illegal for employers to try to persuade us to sign these rights away. This deprives the most desperate of what otherwise might be their only route to a job, for failing that legislation, they might have been able to offer themselves as cheaper labour. This restriction on the individual's freedom to contract is not, however, to be understood just as governments paternalistically protecting us "from ourselves" (though I am not in all circumstances opposed to that). It is also a matter of protecting others from our actions, for when some employees agree to unfavourable terms of employment, this puts pressure on others to accept the same. It can then act as a downward pressure for everyone. If a practice like selling kidneys is allowed to flourish, this does not just increase the options for those in desperate need of money. It also changes the choice set in ways that can significantly reduce options for others. Satz gives the example of kidneys coming to be viewed by local moneylenders as good collateral for loans, and the possibility that those unwilling to sell a kidney would then be denied the opportunity to borrow money.[9] An expansion of choices for some can mean a reduction in choices for others. The easy assumption that banning a practice reduces options is not tenable.

When an obnoxious practice becomes illegal, moreover, this can also be the impetus to the development of more favourable ones. If employers cannot require their workers to work a fourteen-hour day, they may have to introduce machinery that lightens the workload. If they cannot employ cheap child labour, they may have to employ the parents of those child workers at the higher adult rate instead. There are difficult trade-offs between long and short term, and the promise that there will eventually be benefits for all hardly helps those deprived of their immediate employment. But applying this general logic to the current shortage of transplant organs reminds us that shortages do not have to be met just by finding more donors or else introducing markets. If recent medical developments continue, they may also be met by the use of synthetic organs, which can be combined with the patient's own stem cells to minimise the risk of rejection and eliminate the need for immunosuppressive drugs.[10] I have said that my favoured solution for addressing the shortage of organs is a well-advertised and regulated system of presumed consent, with people actively opting out of becoming organ donors rather than opting in. But the solution may ultimately lie in scientific and medical developments that enable us to patch up our bodies without such recourse to either living or dead donors.

If experiments with induced pluripotent stem cells are successful, it may also become possible to dispense with the supplies of human eggs currently required in stem cell research and its potential medical applications. Indeed, if these alternatives do not bear fruit, the prospects for women are gloomy. When Hwang Woo-Suk published his later discredited accounts of success in producing stem cell lines, one of his research collaborators resigned from the team because of concerns about the way the eggs for the process had been acquired.[11] It transpired that many had been purchased (with an average payment of $1,400 to each "donor"), and others "donated" by junior researchers on the team, in ways that aroused serious concerns about the pressures exerted on them. In that research, fewer than two hundred eggs were reportedly used, but considering the process through which these are produced—hyperstimulation of the women's ovaries over a number of days, followed by surgical removal—even that amount is staggering. When we add to this the demand implied in the hoped-for medical applications, the scale of it all begins to look crazy. In *Altruism Reconsidered*, Ingrid Schneider reports that on one conservative estimate—fifty eggs per patient—"every woman in the US aged 18–44 (around 55 million) would have to endure two cycles of ovarian hormone hyperstimulation and then undergo laparoscopic surgery" in order successfully to treat just four of the major diseases—Parkinson's, diabetes, Alzheimer's, ALS—that may be helped by stem cell research.[12] In the light of such estimates, it seems almost beside the point to debate the relative merits of altruistic donation, compensation, and markets. No amount of expansion in the supply of human eggs is going to meet that level of need.

Banning existing markets is problematic, preventing their development where they do not yet exist much less so. But even where markets exist—as they do now in human gametes, though not yet (legally) in human organs—it cannot be assumed that either the desperation, or more moderately, the desires, of those willing to sell are decisive arguments against change. If we take them as such, we could never contemplate employment legislation or antidiscrimination laws. We might also find ourselves committed to a major extension of commodification that later proved medically unnecessary. Unfortunately, in these matters, it is not easy to return to the point of departure.

Policies (b): Payment and Compensation

In chapter three I argued that the contentious issue was markets not money, and that there could be good grounds for making monetary payments to people even while resisting the development of a commercial trade. I also noted, but then left unresolved, some conceptual difficulties about the level of payment and the striking similarity between the "noncommercial" surrogacy industry in the United Kingdom and its overtly commercial counterpart in much of the United States, where the money paid to surrogates seemed much the same. I return now to this issue, though widening it out to include "payments" for bodily tissues and parts.

In a recent report, *Human Bodies: Donation for Medicine and Research*, the Nuffield Council on Bioethics identifies six terms for transactions involving money.[13] *Purchase* is paying a person for a thing: here, we are firmly in the realm of objects, commodities, and markets. But there are forms of payment that fall considerably short of this marketisation. There is *recompense*, defined as "payment to a person in recognition of losses they have incurred, material or otherwise"; this subdivides into *reimbursement*, of the money, for example, spent on train fares getting to a hospital or the income lost through taking days off work, and *compensation*, for nonfinancial losses like inconvenience, discomfort, or time. There is also *reward*, defined as "material advantage gained by a person as a result of donating bodily material, that goes beyond 'recompensing' the person for the losses they have incurred in donating." When reward is calculated as if paying the person a wage, it becomes *remuneration*, and edges close to a purchase. The council is not opposed, in principle, to money payments for people donating human bodily materials but insists on a distinction between *paying for the material* (purchase of a thing) and *paying the people for* their donation. So far as human gametes, for example, are concerned, "the Council rejects outrights the concept of a 'purchase' price for gametes, where any payment made is understood as payment for the gamete itself, rather than as recompense or reward to the donor herself or himself."[14]

These distinctions resonate with my own contrast between payment and compensation as regards surrogacy. In both cases, the object is to draw a firm line between market purchases that treat bodily materials and services as if they were things, and monetary payments that reimburse, compensate, recognise, or reward the person providing the materials or service. Both then beg the question: how do we know when we have crossed that line? Where actual costs incurred are reimbursed, this will be easy enough, but once we also allow compensation for inconvenience, discomfort, and the loss of (normally unpaid) time, or try to recognise the generosity of the donor by provision of some monetary reward, we face the question of what price to put on these. It cannot be a market price—if it is, that defeats the purpose—but since social understandings of worth are shaped by the operations of markets, any notions of fair compensation may, in practice, be closely linked to market prices. This can make the distinctions appear somewhat academic. Fair compensation is implicitly gauged by reference to a market price, but with what then seems an arbitrary amount taken off to ensure the transaction does not become a "market purchase." Regulatory bodies tussling with the appropriate sum to pay a surrogate, for example, or the appropriate compensation for a woman agreeing to undergo egg extraction, are sometimes guided by the idea that the money must not be "too much." It should be high enough to ensure that the person is not worse off as a result of her actions, and where there are significant shortages in supply, high enough to provide an adequate incentive, but it should not be so high as to count as "undue pressure."

This is a common theme as regards surrogates, egg "donors," organ "donors," and participants in medical trials. In all these cases, we hear arguments to the effect that there should be a cap on the amount paid so as to ensure people are not "coerced" by economic circumstances into doing things they would not otherwise do. Concerns about agency and coercion then become the justification for what one might describe—if one thought of exploitation as paying *too little* for a service—as exploitation. In the early 1980s, the New Jersey legislature debated a bill to set a maximum payment to surrogates of $10,000. Other state legislatures, at the time, were debating bills that would have set this as the minimum.[15] In 2011, a woman filed an antitrust lawsuit against the American Society for Reproductive Medicine, arguing that its guidelines on the maximum payable to egg donors (in essence, that over $5,000 per cycle required justification, and that over $10,000 was inappropriate) was keeping prices artificially low.[16] Clearly, there are different understandings at work here of what counts as exploitation.

Just as the Nuffield Council was publishing its report (in 2011), the UK Human Fertilisation and Embryo Authority (HFEA), the regulatory body covering the use of gametes and embryos in fertility treatment and research, announced a change in policy as regards payment to egg donors. It recommended a one-off fee of £750 for each course of egg donation, to replace what had previously been the practice of refunding direct expenses and paying up to £250 for lost earnings. It moved, that is, from what the Nuffield Council describes as reimbursement to a fixed-rate compensation. Requiring egg donors to produce a bundle of receipts was seen as somewhat insulting, while paying only for lost earnings was unfair to those not currently in employment, who were still giving up their time. More pragmatically, the HFEA was concerned about the growth in "reproductive tourism" and the traffic of people seeking assisted reproduction in Spanish clinics, where payments of €900 were ensuring a more ready supply of eggs.[17] Compared with the $5,000 routinely paid to egg donors in the United States, and the $50,000 reputedly offered in one US college newspaper,[18] £750 is not a great deal of money, but a number of commentators view it as moving too far towards paying for gametes.

My own (somewhat reluctant) view is that it *is* acceptable, and not a major change from the previous regime. But the actual amount is either arbitrary or set to match the Spanish payment, and if the latter, simulates a competitive market. Once payment goes beyond the reimbursement of direct expenditure, it becomes impossible to attach a monetary price to people's activities without in some way deriving one's information from existing markets, and the firm line between paying for a thing and paying people for their assistance becomes somewhat blurred. On this issue, I do not have clear answers. I agree with the Nuffield Council that there are distinctions in principle, but I suspect that most of the practical applications will overlap more closely with market solutions than those pursuing them hope. On a more confident note, I would stress that the difficulties attending this are not so different in kind from those that arise when deciding when a person has died, at what age a child is mature enough to take major life decisions, or any number of related issues in which we have to exercise judgment. Principled distinctions only go so far. Practical implementation necessarily involves judgment.

Conclusion

As the arguments developed in this book demonstrate, the relationship between markets, bodies, and property is complex, and sometimes almost perverse. Those who model rape on a violation of property are not thereby committed to any particular views on whether sexuality should be up for sale. Those who sell bodily services sometimes call on notions of body ownership to explain their choice of occupation and assert their control, but often repudiate the language of renting or deny that they had much choice. Those who insist on the virtues of body ownership in debates about the commercial exploitation of body products and parts are as likely to be the opponents of commercialisation as its advocates. The complexities of the relationship undermine any straightforward thesis about property claims implying metaphorical commodification or metaphorical commodification encouraging actual commodification. Applying property language to the body diminishes distinctions between bodies and "other material resources," and to the extent that it focuses attention on individuals and individual choice, also narrows down the relevant range of considerations in the making of public policy. But we cannot simply say that thinking of yourself as in a relationship of ownership to your body makes it more likely that you will put it up for sale.

What I do, however, claim is that both actual and metaphorical commodification matter, that markets change things, and so too does thinking ourselves as in a relationship of ownership to our bodies and selves. The body is not sacrosanct, and since we take the body with us in everything we do, we cannot simply say "the body is special" and leave it at that. Some of the arguments I have put forward against the commercialisation of intimate bodily services rely on features they share with all forms of employment; some of my argument, therefore, refuses any simple dividing line between body and not-body to focus on what happens at the outer edges of a continuum. But I have also made claims about the body as what potentially alerts us to what we share, and I argued that our status as equals is the potential casualty when the bodies of some are routinely employed to patch up problems with the bodies of others.

Developments in medical science are going to offer increasing opportunities for this, and the more the opportunities the greater the "shortage." Nancy Scheper-Hughes argues that "the very idea of organ or kidney 'scarcity' is what Ivan Illich would call an artificially created need, one that is invented by transplant technicians, doctors and their brokers, and dangled before the eyes of an ever expanding sick, aging, desperate and dying population."[19] It's not that the sick and dying on transplant waiting lists, or the infertile couples desperately searching for the means to have a child, are making up their misery, but it is only when medical technology has offered a way of circumventing this that we can sensibly talk of a "need" or identify a "shortage." It is only, moreover, by restricting whom we designate by "those in need," limiting it to "those in need and with the necessary cash," that we can fool ourselves that the introduction of commercial markets can solve the shortage. If we consider the problem of infertility at the level of the world as a whole (and infertility can be an especially acute problem in societies where it can mean repudiation or even death), it becomes immediately apparent that there cannot be enough surrogates to go around. Commercial surrogacy only "solves" the problem of infertility if we limit our definition of the infertile to those who can afford to pay. Similarly, if we consider all those the world over who could benefit from an organ transplant, and then add in the unknown millions who would be able to benefit from the new kinds of transplant that are no doubt being worked on, it becomes apparent that there cannot be enough donors (paid or unpaid) to go around. Ingrid Schneider's estimate of the number of human eggs that would be necessary to treat four major diseases paints an impossible picture just for the United States: think of that as applied the world over. The idea that markets in surrogacy and eggs and human organs can solve existing shortages makes sense only if we limit our attention to those who are not only in need but also have the money to pay.

I have argued that there is a social cost to these markets, beyond the individual costs that may bear on those who sell, and particularly so in the most stark version of a body market, where people are trading in live human organs. In that market, inequality is both cause and consequence. Inequality is the only plausible reason why some are in a position to buy and others feel the need to sell, and equality is the likely casualty, for it is hard to sustain notions of ourselves as equals when the bodies of some are being employed to solve problems in the bodies of others.

Carole Pateman remarked in 2002 that "where lines are to be drawn about property and commodification, what should be alienable and inalienable, and where the balance should be between the two, are some of the most pressing issues of the new century."[20] If there is one thing we can be sure of, it is that the number and difficulty of these issues is going to continue to multiply. Seeking to preempt those difficulties by individualised assertions of our property rights in our bodies is not, I have argued, the best way to go. We need to consider very carefully the risks associated with regarding our bodies as property and the threat to principles of human equality when we routinely send bodies to market.

Notes

Introduction

1. Nir Eyal, "Is the Body Special?" *Utilitas* 21, no. 2 (2009): 233–45.

2. Margaret Jane Radin, *Contested Commodities: The Trouble with Trade in Sex, Children, Body Parts and Other Things* (Cambridge, MA: Harvard University Press, 1996); Debra Satz, *Why Some Things Should Not Be For Sale: The Moral Limits of Markets* (Oxford and New York: Oxford University Press, 2010); Michael J. Sandel, *What Money Can't Buy: The Moral Limits of Markets* (New York and London: Allen Lane, 2012).

3. Baby markets are suggested as a solution to baby shortages in E. M. Landes and R. A. Posner, "The Economics of the Baby Shortage," *Journal of Legal Studies* 7 (1978): 323–48; it's not clear whether this is a playful or real suggestion.

4. As described in Nancy Scheper-Hughes, "Commodity Fetishism in Organs Trafficking," *Body and Society* 7, no. 2–3 (2001): 1–8.

5. I am aware that my pairing of prostitution and commercial surrogacy will be seen as offensive to some and analytically mistaken to others, but I follow Carole Pateman in *The Sexual Contract* (Cambridge: Polity Press, 1988), in seeing both activities as implying an understanding of the self and body as property.

6. James Meikle, "Kidney Transplants and Cancer: The Risks," *The Guardian*, March 22, 2011.

7. Julian Savulescu, "Is the Sale of Body Parts Wrong?" *Journal of Medical Ethics* 29 (2003): 138–39, at 138. Other cases for relaxing the prohibitions on human organ sales include Janet Radcliffe Richards et al., "The Case for Allowing Kidney Sales," *The Lancet* 351 (1998): 1950–52; Janet Radcliffe Richards, *The Ethics of Transplants: Why Careless Thought Costs Lives* (Oxford: Oxford University Press, 2012); and Charles A. Erin and John Harris, "A Monopsonistic Market: Or How to Buy and Sell Human Organs, Tissues and Cells Ethically," in *Life and Death under High Technology Medicine*, ed. Ian Robinson (Manchester: Manchester University Press, 1994), 134–53.

8. John Locke, *Second Treatise on Government*, 1690. Chapter V, Section 27. The distinction between property in the person and the body is convincingly argued in Jeremy Waldron, *The Right to Private Property* (Oxford: Clarendon Press, 1988); Donna Dickenson, *Property, Women, and Politics* (Cambridge: Polity Press, 1997); and Janet Coleman, "Pre-Modern Property and Self-Ownership before and after Locke; or, When Did Common Decency Become a Private Rather Than a Public Virtue?" *European Journal of Political Theory* 4, no. 2 (2005): 125–45.

9. 1 Cor. 6:19–20 (New King James Version Bible).

10. Arlie R. Hochschild, *The Managed Heart: Commercialization of Human Feeling* (Berkeley: University of California Press, 1983).

11. Sandel, *What Money Can't Buy*, 112.

12. Ibid., 113.

13. This is an important part of what Carole Pateman argues in *The Sexual Contract*.

14. Heather Widdows, "Rejecting the Choice Paradigm: Rethinking the Ethical Framework in Prostitution and Egg Sale Debates," in *Gender, Agency, and Coercion*, ed. Sumi Madhok, Anne Phillips, and Kalpana Wilson (Basingstoke: Palgrave Macmillan, 2013).

15. Carol Wolkowitz, *Bodies at Work* (London: Sage, 2006), 21.

16. Sandel, *What Money Can't Buy*, 33.

17. Martha C. Nussbaum, "'Whether from Reason or Prejudice': Taking Money for Bodily Services," in *Sex and Social Justice* (New York: Oxford University Press, 1999).

18. This is more the implication Carol Wolkowitz or Julia O'Connell Davidson take from the continuum between prostitution and other forms of body work: not that prostitution is therefore okay, but that that other forms of work are also problematic. Wolkowitz, *Bodies at Work*; Julia O'Connell Davidson, "The Rights and Wrongs of Prostitution," *Hypatia* 17, no. 2 (2002): 84–98.

19. See, for example, many of the essays in Martha M. Ertman and Joan C. Williams, eds., *Rethinking Commodification: Cases and Readings in Law and Culture* (New York: New York University Press, 2005); and Peter Halewood, "On Commodification and Self-Ownership," *Yale Journal of Law and the Humanities* 20 (2008): 131–62.

20. Including Halewood, "On Commodification and Self-Ownership"; Nils Hoppe, *Bioequity: Property and the Human Body* (Aldershot: Ashgate, 2009); Remigius Nwabueze, *Biotechnology and the Challenge of*

Property: Property Rights in Dead Bodies, Body Parts, and Genetic Information (Aldershot: Ashgate, 2007).

21. Carol M. Rose, "Whither Commodification?" in Ertman and Williams, *Rethinking Commodification*, 421. Although not herself so entirely converted to the empowering nature of commodification, she gives the example of the siting of sewage treatment plants. If a reverse auction were established, with the level of compensation going up until some neighbourhood agrees to take it, it will almost certainly be the poorer neighbourhoods that end up hosting the plant. But this is what happens already, because those in richer neighbourhoods have the power and contacts to ensure that their interests are well protected. The first best solution would be perfect equity. "But in a second-best world where there actually are implicit markets, all-out commodification might just start to look more attractive—more attractive that is, than the fake processes that disguise the market, drain off the money to intermediaries, and let the most disadvantaged parties hang out to dry." Rose, "Whither Commodification?," 407.

22. This was one of the issues in *Regina v. Kelly and Lindsay* (C.A.) [1998] 3 All E.R. 741. I discuss this case briefly in chapter four.

23. For recent developments in jurisprudence that begin to modify the no-property rule for both live and dead body parts, see Nwabueze, *Biotechnology and the Challenge of Property*; and Hoppe, *Bioequity: Property and the Human Body*.

24. As argued in Laura Brace, *The Politics of Property: Labour, Freedom, and Belonging* (Edinburgh: Edinburgh University Press, 2004).

25. I take this example from Eyal, "Is the Body Special?," 237.

26. J. W. Harris, "Who Owns My Body?" *Oxford Journal of Legal Studies* 16, no. 1 (1996): 55–84, at 65.

27. Lisa C. Ikemoto, "Eggs as Capital: Human Egg Procurement in the Fertility Industry and the Stem Cell Research Enterprise," *Signs* 34, no. 4 (2009): 763–81, at 779.

Chapter One

1. "What peculiarly signifies the situation of woman is that she—a free and autonomous being like all human creatures—nevertheless finds herself living in a world where men compel her to assume the

status of the Other. They propose to stabilise her as an object." Simone de Beauvoir, *The Second Sex* (London: Vintage, 1997), 29.

2. Jonathan Quong, "Left-Libertarianism: Rawlsian not Luck Egalitarian," *Journal of Political Philosophy* 19, no. 1 (2011): 64–89, at 87.

3. For a compilation of the more radical versions, see Peter Vallentyne and Hillel Steiner, eds., *The Origins of Left-Libertarianism: An Anthology of Historical Writings* (New York: Palgrave, 2000); and Peter Vallentyne and Hillel Steiner, eds., *Left-Libertarianism and Its Critics: The Contemporary Debate* (New York: Palgrave, 2000).

4. Rosalind Pollack Petchesky, "The Body as Property: A Feminist Re-Vision," in *Conceiving the New World Order: The Global Politics of Reproduction, ed.* Faye D Ginsburg and Rayna Rapp (Berkeley: University of California Press, 1995), 387–406.

5. Ngaire Naffine, "The Legal Standing of Self-Ownership: Or the Self-Possessed Man and the Woman Possessed," *Journal of Law and Society* 25, no. 2 (1998): 193–212, at 198. The description occurs in the context of a robust critique of self-ownership.

6. Harris "Who Owns My Body?," 55.

7. Immanuel Kant, *Lectures on Ethics* (Cambridge: Cambridge University Press, 1992), 165.

8. Georg Lukács, *History and Class Consciousness* (1922; London: Merlin Press, 1968), 100.

9. Pateman, *The Sexual Contract*; Carole Pateman, "Self-Ownership and Property in the Person: Democratization and a Tale of Two Concepts," *Journal of Political Philosophy* 10, no. 1 (2002): 20–53.

10. Pateman, *The Sexual Contract*, 216.

11. Jennifer Nedelsky, "Property in Potential Life? A Relational Approach to Choosing Legal Categories," *Canadian Journal of Law and Jurisprudence* 6, no. 2 (1993): 343–66. See also "Reconceiving Autonomy," *Yale Journal of Law and Feminism* 1 (1989): 7–36; "Law, Boundaries, and the Bounded Self," *Representations* 30 (1993); "Are Persons Property?" *Adelaide Law Review* 24 (2003): 123–31; all by Nedelsky.

12. Radin, *Contested Commodities*, 88.

13. Martha C. Nussbaum, "Objectification," *Philosophy and Public Affairs* 24, no. 4 (1995): 249–91, at 257.

14. Radin, *Contested Commodities*, 13.

15. Stephen Wilkinson, *Bodies for Sale: Ethics and Exploitation in the Human Body Trade* (London: Routledge, 2003), 46.

16. Carole Pateman argues that it is more precise to talk of property in the person than self-ownership, and that "ownership" obscures crucial questions about alienability, inalienability, and contract that are better foregrounded when we acknowledge that property is at stake. Pateman, "Self-Ownership and Property in the Person," 20–53, at 21.

17. It "seems to describe not only autonomy or a right to maintain the sacred wholeness of one's person or body, but also the opposite of this, that is, the capacity of a person as transactor to deal in his own body or person as commodity." Halewood, "On Commodification and Self-Ownership," 134.

18. Including Carole Pateman, Jennifer Nedelsky, Christine Overall, and Heather Widdows.

19. Martha M. Ertman and Joan C. Williams, eds., *Rethinking Commodification: Cases and Readings in Law and Culture* (New York: New York University Press, 2005), arguing the potential benefits of commodification for the socially and politically marginal, is very much a feminist inflected collection. See also Nancy Folbre on the widespread feeling that paying for care taints something that ought to be provided (by women) as an activity of love: *The Invisible Heart: Economics and Family Values* (New York: New Press, 2001); *Who Pays for the Kids? Gender and the Structures of Constraint* (London and New York: Routledge, 1996).

20. Katherine Silbaugh, "Commodification and Women's Household Labor," in Ertman and Williams, *Rethinking Commodification*, 299.

21. Nussbaum, "Whether from Reason or Prejudice"; see also Satz, *Why Some Things Should Not Be For Sale*; Cécile Fabre's *Whose Body Is It Anyway?* (New York: Oxford University Press, 2006), is not an explicitly feminist work, but expresses similar reservations.

22. The extensive literature includes Nussbaum, "Whether from Reason or Prejudice"; Satz, "Markets in Women's Sexual Labor," *Ethics* 106 (1995): 63–85; Catharine A. MacKinnon, "Prostitution and Civil Rights," *Michigan Journal of Gender and Law* 1 (1993): 13–31; Julia O'Connell Davidson, "The Rights and Wrongs of Prostitution," *Hypatia* 17, no. 2 (2002): 84–98; Kathy Miriam, "Stopping the Traffic in Women: Power, Agency, and Abolition in Feminist Debates over Sex Trafficking," *Journal of Social Philosophy* 36, no. 1 (2005): 1–17;

Rutvica Andrijasevic, *Migration, Agency, and Citizenship in Sex Trafficking* (New York: Palgrave Macmillan, 2010).

23. I have mostly adopted prostitution to refer to the institution, and sex workers to refer to the people involved in the trade. This better captures my own emphasis on the continuities of different forms of work and my concern to stress the agency even of those making their choices under highly constrained conditions, while leaving space for an argument about prostitution and commercial surrogacy nonetheless being different.

24. Nussbaum, "Whether from Reason or Prejudice," 283.

25. Carmel Shalev, *Birth Power: The Case for Surrogacy* (New Haven, CT: Yale University Press, 1989).

26. See, for example, Elizabeth Grosz, *Volatile Bodies* (Bloomington: Indiana University Press, 1994); Moira Gatens, *Imaginary Bodies: Ethics, Power, and Corporeality* (London: Routledge, 1996); Toril Moi, *What Is a Woman? And Other Essays* (Oxford: Oxford University Press, 1999); Iris M. Young, *On Female Body Experience: Throwing Like a Girl and Other Essays* (Oxford: Oxford University Press, 2005); Sonia Kruks, *Retrieving Experience* (Ithaca, NY: Cornell University Press, 2001).

27. For example, Anne Phillips, *The Politics of Presence* (Oxford: Oxford University Press, 1995); Nirmal Puwar, *Space Invaders: Race, Gender, and Bodies Out of Place* (Oxford: Berg, 2004).

28. Influential feminist critiques of mind/body dualism include Genevieve Lloyd, *The Man of Reason: "Male" and "Female" in Western Philosophy* (London: Methuen, 1986); and Raia Prokhovnik, *Rational Woman: A Feminist Critique of Dichotomy* (London: Routledge, 1999).

29. Ngaire Naffine, "The Legal Status of Self-Ownership: Or the Self-Possessed Man and the Woman Possessed," *Journal of Law and Society* 25, no. 2 (1988): 193–212, at 202. Naffine provides a number of illustrations of this from the literature. To my mind, she effectively challenges G. A. Cohen's claim that the self in the thesis of self-ownership is merely reflexive, implying no internal division between owner and that which is owned.

30. Ronald Dworkin, "Comment on Narveson: In Defence of Equality," *Social Philosophy and Policy* 1 (1983): 24–40, at 39. In *Whose Body Is It Anyway?*, Cécile Fabre rejects this prophylactic line and argues that egalitarianism does indeed imply a right to confiscate unused or excess body parts for the benefit of those less favoured.

31. Nussbaum, "Whether from Reason or Prejudice," 276.

32. "A weak property right involves only a choice to transfer gratuitously. A strong property right involves a choice to transfer for value." Stephen R. Munzer, *A Theory of Property* (Cambridge: Cambridge University Press, 1990), 49.

33. John Christman, *The Myth of Property: Toward an Egalitarian Theory of Ownership* (New York and Oxford: Oxford University Press, 1994).

34. Laura Brace, *The Politics of Property: Labour, Freedom, and Belonging* (New York: Palgrave Macmillan, 2004).

35. Including Dickenson, *Property, Women, and Politics*; Brace, *The Politics of Property*; Christman, *The Myth of Property*.

36. Wesley Newcomb Hohfeld, "Fundamental Legal Conceptions as Applied in Judicial Reasoning," *Yale Law Journal* 26, no. 8 (1917): 710–70; A. M. Honoré, "Ownership," in *Oxford Essays in Jurisprudence*, ed. A. G. Guest (Oxford: Oxford University Press, 1961).

37. *Moore v. Regents of the University of California* (51 Cal. 3d 120, Supreme Court of California, 1990).

38. Cited in Halewood, "On Commodification and Self-Ownership," 150–51.

39. Dickenson, *Property, Women, and Politics*.

40. Ibid., 79.

41. Donna Dickenson, *Property in the Body: Feminist Perspectives* (Cambridge: Cambridge University Press, 2007), 68.

42. Dickenson, *Property in the Body*, chap. 3.

43. Pateman, "Self-Ownership and Property in the Person," 33.

44. Nussbaum, "Whether from Reason or Prejudice," 291.

45. I am influenced here by Harry Braverman's reading of Marx in *Labor and Monopoly Capital: The Degradation of Work in the Twentieth Century* (New York and London: Monthly Review Press, 1974).

46. Philip Pettit, *Republicanism: A Theory of Freedom and Government* (Oxford: Oxford University Press, 1999).

47. Radin, *Contested Commodities*, 93.

48. Lynn Hunt, *Inventing Human Rights* (New York: W. W. Norton, 2007).

49. Specifically, Hunt argues that the possibility of thinking like this was enhanced in eighteenth-century Europe by the rise of the novel. As reading became more and more an appeal to the sentiments, evoking feelings of dread, horror, and pity, readers were encouraged to identify

with the plight of the hero or heroine, and to recognise a commonality with people who would otherwise never enter their world. Her argument tells a story of human rights that locates its origins squarely in America and Europe. For a telling critique of what he sees as Hunt's "creation myth," see Samuel Moyn, *The Last Utopia: Human Rights in History* (Cambridge, MA: Harvard University Press, 2010).

50. Hunt, *Inventing Human Rights*, 82.

51. Ibid., 112.

52. Judith Butler, *Frames of War: When Is Life Grievable?* (London: Verso, 2009).

53. Joanna Bourke, *What It Means to Be Human* (New York: Little, Brown, 2011).

54. B. Björkman and S. O. Hansson, "Bodily Rights and Property Rights," *Journal of Medical Ethics* 32, no. 4 (2006): 209–14, at 211.

55. Petchesky, "The Body as Property: A Feminist Re-Vision," 397.

56. Munzer, *A Theory of Property*.

57. As Jennifer Nedelsky argues in her discussion of Petchesky and Carole Rose in her discussion of Munzer. Nedelsky, "Property in Potential Life?"; Carol M. Rose, *Property and Persuasion: Essays on the History, Theory, and Rhetoric of Ownership* (Boulder, CO: Westview Press, 1994), 51.

58. Robert Nozick, *Anarchy, State, and Utopia* (New York: Harper and Row, 1974); G. A. Cohen, *Self-Ownership, Freedom, and Equality* (Cambridge: Cambridge University Press, 1995). Cohen initially viewed self-ownership as a necessary underpinning to a Marxist theory of exploitation that talks of the "theft" of the worker's labour time, but later came to see it as incompatible with socialism.

59. Cohen, *Self-Ownership, Freedom, and Equality*, 214, 215.

60. See also Alasdair Cochrane, "Ownership and Justice for Animals," *Utilitas* 21, no. 4 (2009): 424–42, for a critique of Cohen's understanding of ownership.

61. Harris, "Who Owns My Body?," 65.

Chapter Two

1. Louise du Toit, *A Philosophical Investigation of Rape: The Making and Unmaking of the Feminine Self* (New York and London: Routledge, 2009), 35.

2. Du Toit points to 1481 as the first written record of this in England: *Philosophical Investigation of Rape*, 36.

3. Susan Brownmiller, *Against Our Will: Men, Women, and Rape* (New York: Simon and Schuster, 1975), 85.

4. Jane E. Larson, "Women Understand So Little, They Call My Good Nature 'Deceit': A Feminist Rethinking of Seduction," *Columbia Law Review* 93, no. 2 (1993): 375–472.

5. Lorenne M. G. Clark and Debra J. Lewis, *Rape: The Price of Coercive Sexuality* (Toronto: The Women's Press, 1977), 119.

6. Nicola Lacey, "Unspeakable Subjects, Impossible Rights: Sexuality, Integrity, and Criminal Law," *Canadian Journal of Law and Jurisprudence* 11, no. 1 (1998): 47–68, at 59.

7. I draw here particularly on the work of Jennifer Nedelsky, "Reconceiving Autonomy"; "Law, Boundaries, and the Bounded Self"; "Property in Potential Life? A Relational Approach to Choosing Legal Categories"; "Violence against Women: Challenges to the Liberal State and Relational Feminism," in *Political Order*, ed. Ian Shapiro and Russell Hardin, Nomos 38 (New York: New York University Press, 1995), 454–97; and "Are Persons Property?"

8. C. B. Macpherson, *The Political Theory of Possessive Individualism* (Oxford: Clarendon Press, 1962); Pateman, *The Sexual Contract*.

9. Alexandra Wald, "What's Rightfully Ours: Toward a Property Theory of Rape," *Columbia Journal of Law and Social Problems* 30 (1996–67): 459–502, at 461, 475. Wald calls on Margaret Radin and Marilyn Strathern to support a claim about women needing to be recognised as property holders in order to be recognised as persons. In my reading, her arguments resonate more closely with those of Donna Dickenson in *Property, Women, and Politics* (Cambridge: Polity Press, 1997).

10. Catharine MacKinnon, *Toward a Feminist Theory of the State* (Cambridge, MA: Harvard University Press, 1989), 173.

11. Donald A. Dripps, "Beyond Rape: An Essay on the Difference between the Presence of Force and the Absence of Consent," *Columbia Law Review* 92 (1992): 1780–809.

12. I have tried to avoid using the term *victim*, which is criticised in much of the feminist literature on rape, but at many points in this chapter I have found it difficult to come up with an alternative.

13. Dripps, "Beyond Rape," 1789.

14. Robin West, "Legitimating the Illegitimate: A Comment on 'Beyond Rape,'" *Columbia Law Review* 93 (1993): 1456.

15. West, "Legitimating the Illegitimate," 1448.

16. Alan Wertheimer, *Consent to Sexual Relations* (Cambridge: Cambridge University Press, 2003), 34.

17. Richard Posner, *Sex and Reason* (Cambridge, MA: Harvard University Press, 1992), 388.

18. David Archard, "The Wrong of Rape," *Philosophical Quarterly* 57, no. 228 (2007): 374–93. Archard himself defines rape as nonconsensual sex, but he argues that we must understand this as "sex-without-consent," a qualitatively distinct experience from consensual sex.

19. Nicola Lacey, "Unspeakable Subjects, Impossible Rights: Sexuality, Integrity, and Criminal Law," *Canadian Journal of Law and Jurisprudence* 11, no. 1 (1998): 47–68, at 59. Lacey notes that the repression of the body in legal doctrine typically combines with an almost pornographic focus on the body in the conduct of rape trials, but this is clearly no compensation.

20. Monique Plaza, "Our Damages and Their Compensation, Rape: The Will Not to Know of Michel Foucault," *Feminist Issues* 1, no. 2 (1981): 29. French edition 1978. The panel discussion is reproduced as "Confinement, Psychiatry, Power," in Lawrence D. Kritzman, ed., *Politics, Philosophy, Culture: Interviews and Other Writings, 1972–1984*, by Michel Foucault (New York and London: Routledge, 1988).

21. Wertheimer, *Consent to Sexual Relations*: 33.

22. Michael Davis, "Setting Penalties: What Does Rape Deserve?" *Law and Philosophy* 3, no. 1 (1984): 61–110, at 62.

23. Davis, "Setting Penalties," 105.

24. Clark and Lewis, *Rape: The Price of Coercive Sexuality*, 168–79. They argue that treating rape as an attack on female sexuality reproduces property-related ideas of rape as reducing the value of the woman. They also argue that it falsely represents rape as a *sexual* act, making it impossible for people to register the assault and harm in a so-called nonviolent rape.

25. Brownmiller, *Against Our Will*, 379n, quoted in Davis, "Setting Penalties," at 110.

26. "Confinement, Psychiatry, Power," in Kritzman, *Politics, Philosophy, Culture: Interviews and Other Writings, 1972–1984*, by Michel Foucault, 200. As regards the second issue, of sexual relations between adults and children, he was inclined to say that "from the moment that a child doesn't refuse, there is no reason to punish any act," 204.

27. H. E. Baber, "How Bad Is Rape?" *Hypatia* 2, no. 2 (1987): 125–38.

28. Baber, "How Bad Is Rape?," 134, 136.

29. Joan McGregor, *Is It Rape? On Acquaintance Rape and Taking Women's Consent Seriously* (Aldershot: Ashgate, 2005), 221–22.

30. McGregor, *Is It Rape?*, 222.

31. Sharon Marcus, "Fighting Bodies, Fighting Words: A Theory and Politics of Rape Prevention," in *Feminists Theorize the Political*, ed. Judith Butler and Joan W. Scott (New York and London: Routledge, 1992), 398.

32. Nedelsky, "Reconceiving Autonomy," 12.

33. Ibid.

34. Nedelsky, "Law, Boundaries, and the Bounded Self," 168.

35. Ibid., 170. Elsewhere she notes the initial oddity in this: "Isn't rape quintessentially about boundary violation and don't women desperately need better protection for the boundaries of their persons? Isn't this is of all places where we need to claim the same kind of boundary protection men get?" Nedelsky, "Violence against Women," 474.

36. Nedelsky, "Violence against Women," 475.

37. Susan J. Brison, *Aftermath: Violence and the Remaking of a Self* (Princeton, NJ: Princeton University Press, 2003).

38. Margrit Shildrick, *Leaky Bodies and Boundaries: Feminism, Postmodernism, and (Bio)ethics* (New York and London: Routledge, 1997).

39. See also Ann J. Cahill, *Rethinking Rape* (Ithaca, NY: Cornell University Press, 2001), for a similar emphasis on embodied experience.

40. Arguments that stress the assault on personhood include Archard, "The Wrong of Rape"; Joan McGregor, "Force, Consent, and the Reasonable Woman," in *In Harm's Way: Essays in Honor of Joel Feinberg*, ed. Jules L Coleman and Allen Buchanan (Cambridge: Cambridge University Press, 1994), 231–54; and Jean Hampton, "Defining Wrong and Defining Rape," in *A Most Detestable Crime: New Philosophical Essays on Rape*, ed. Keith Burgess-Jackson (New York and Oxford: Oxford University Press, 1999).

41. Archard, "The Wrong of Rape," 390.

42. Ibid., 391.

43. When Joan McGregor claims the centrality of sex and sexual expression to personal identity, she acknowledges that how we define personhood may differ culturally. Somewhat unsatisfactorily, she brushes this aside, observing that it is not an objection, "since what

we are concerned about is a criminal code for this culture." McGregor, "Force, Consent, and the Reasonable Woman," 234.

44. We may not talk so easily if the person who attacks us is a family member or someone we know, but there, too, the analogy with rape is imperfect. Women raped by strangers do not therefore find it easier to recount their experiences.

45. Hampton, "Defining Wrong and Defining Rape," 138.

46. Wertheimer, *Consent to Sexual Relations*, 103.

47. Ibid., 113.

48. Ibid., 117–18. He is arguing here against Baber and Jeffrie G. Murphy, "Some Ruminations on Women, Violence, and the Criminal Law," in Coleman and Buchanan, *In Harm's Way*, 209–30. Murphy suggests that if the theory of female sexuality that renders rape the most serious of all assaults turns out to disadvantage women in other contexts, maybe we should try to change it.

49. Joanna Bourke, *Rape: A History from 1860 to the Present Day* (London: Virago, 2007), 407.

50. Bourke, *Rape: A History from 1860 to the Present Day*, 426.

51. Camille Paglia, *Sex, Art, and American Culture* (New York: Vintage, 1992); Katie Roiphe, *The Morning After: Sex, Fear and Feminism on Campus* (Boston: Little, Brown, 1993).

52. Marcus, "Fighting Bodies, Fighting Words," 387.

53. Carine M. Mardorossian, "Toward a New Feminist Theory of Rape," *Signs* 27, no. 3 (2002): 743–75.

54. Susan J. Brison, "Outliving Oneself: Trauma, Memory, and Personal Identity," in *Feminists Rethink the Self*, ed. Diana Tietjen Meyers (Boulder, CO: Westview Press, 1997), 17.

55. Rachel Hall, " 'It Can Happen to You': Rape Prevention in the Age of Risk Management," *Hypatia* 19, no. 3 (2004): 1–19, at 11.

56. West, "Legitimating the Illegitimate." 1448.

Chapter Three

1. For example, in Joanna Phoenix's study of sex workers in the United Kingdom. Joanna Phoenix, *Making Sense of Prostitution* (New York: St. Martin's Press, 1999).

2. In parts of India, surrogacy is stigmatised because it is regarded as a form of prostitution, and this stigma is one of the major difficulties

surrogates face. Amrita Pande, "'At Least I Am Not Sleeping with Anyone': Resisting the Stigma of Commercial Surrogacy in India," *Feminist Studies* 36, no. 2 (2010): 292–312.

3. Amrita Pande, "Commercial Surrogacy in India: Manufacturing a Perfect Mother-Worker," *Signs* 35, no. 4 (2010): 971.

4. For a discussion of the Israeli Surrogate Motherhood Agreements Law (1996), see Pamela Laufer-Ukeles, "Gestation: Work for Hire or the Essence of Motherhood? A Comparative Legal Analysis," *Duke Journal of Gender Law and Policy* 9 (2002): 91–134.

5. Laufer-Ukeles, "Gestation: Work for Hire or the Essence of Motherhood?," 91–134.

6. See Karen Busby and Delaney Vun, "Revisiting The Handmaid's Tale: Feminist Theory Meets Empirical Research on Surrogate Mothers," *Canadian Journal of Family Law*, 26, no. 1 (2010): 13–94, for a survey of current legislation and court judgments in the United States, United Kingdom, and Canada; and Lisa Ikemoto, "Reproductive Tourism: Equality Concerns in the Global Market for Fertility Services," *Law and Inequality* 27 (2009): 277–309, for an overview of developments in the global market.

7. Lawrence Stone, *New York Times*, April 5, 1987. Cited in Pateman, *The Sexual Contract*, 211.

8. Pande, "Commercial Surrogacy in India," 979.

9. Pande, "Resisting the Stigma of Commercial Surrogacy in India," 301–3.

10. Andrijasevic, *Migration, Agency, and Citizenship in Sex Trafficking*, 121.

11. Uma Narayan, "The 'Gift' of a Child: Commercial Surrogacy, Gift Surrogacy, and Motherhood," in *Expecting Trouble: Surrogacy, Fetal Abuse, and New Reproductive Technologies*, ed. Patricia Boling (Boulder, CO: Westview Press, 1995), 177–201.

12. For example, Gena Corea, *The Mother Machine: Reproductive Technologies from Artificial Insemination to Artificial Wombs* (New York: Harper and Row, 1985). See also the discussion in Anne Donchin, "Feminist Critiques of New Fertility Technologies: Implications for Social Policy," *Journal of Medicine and Philosophy* 21 (1996): 475–98.

13. E. M. Landes and R. A. Posner, "The Economics of the Baby Shortage," *Journal of Legal Studies* 7 (June 1978): 323–48; see also Richard A. Posner, "The Ethics of Enforcing Contracts of Surrogate Motherhood," *Journal of Contemporary Health Law and Policy* 5 (1989): 21–31.

14. Christine Overall, *Human Reproduction: Principles, Practices, Policies* (Toronto and Oxford: Oxford University Press), 123.

15. Helena Ragoné, *Surrogate Motherhood: Conception in the Heart* (Boulder, CO: Westview Press, 1994), 17.

16. Laura Purdy, for example, defends commercial surrogacy arrangements but argues that the woman should be paid even if the baby is stillborn. Laura M. Purdy, *Reproducing Persons: Issues in Feminist Bioethics* (Ithaca, NY: Cornell University Press, 1996), 195.

17. Elizabeth S. Anderson, "Is Women's Labor a Commodity?" *Philosophy and Public Affairs* 19, no. 1 (1990): 71–92; Radin, *Contested Commodities*.

18. Anderson, "Is Women's Labor a Commodity?," 77.

19. Overall, *Human Reproduction: Principles, Practices, Policies*, 124.

20. Ragoné, *Surrogate Motherhood: Conception in the Heart*; Busby and Vun, "Revisiting The Handmaid's Tale."

21. Ragoné, *Surrogate Motherhood: Conception in the Heart*, 14; Purdy, *Reproducing Persons: Issues in Feminist Bioethics*.

22. Michael J. Sandel, *The Case against Perfectionism* (Cambridge, MA: Belknap Press of Harvard University Press, 2007).

23. *In the Matter of Baby M*, 217 N.J. Super 313 (Ch.Div. 1987).

24. *In re Baby M*, 537 A.2d. 1227 (N.J. 1988).

25. When she turned eighteen, Melissa Stern ("M") terminated Whitehead's parental rights and arranged to be adopted by the woman she regarded as her mother, Elizabeth Stern.

26. Defenders of enforceable contracts included Shalev, *Birth Power: The Case for Surrogacy*; and Lori B. Andrews, "Surrogate Motherhood: The Challenge for Feminists," in *The Ethics of Reproductive Technology*, ed. Kenneth D. Alpern (New York and Oxford: Oxford University Press, 1992), 205–19.

27. Marjorie Schultz, "Reproductive Technology and Intent-Based Parenthood: An Opportunity for Gender Neutrality," *Wisconsin Law Review* (1990): 297–398, at 354–55.

28. Shalev, *Birth Power: The Case for Surrogacy*, 165.

29. For a critical account of agency in feminist thinking, see Madhok, Phillips, and Wilson, *Gender, Agency, and Coercion*.

30. Satz, *Why Some Things Should Not Be For Sale*, 117–21.

31. Mary Lyndon Shanley, "'Surrogate Mothering' and Women's Freedom: A Critique of Contracts for Human Reproduction," *Signs* 18 (1993): 618–39, at 628.

32. Physical detachability is not, of course, the only consideration in determining what kind of contracts can be legitimately enforced. In chapter four, I consider markets in bodily products and parts that are by definition detachable: if they were not, you could only get them by killing the source. In these cases, the fact of detachability clearly does not settle the desirability of the market.

33. Ikemoto, "Reproductive Tourism: Equality Concerns in the Global Market for Fertility Services," 277–309, at 306.

34. Elly Teman, "The Medicalization of 'Nature' in the 'Artificial Body': Surrogate Motherhood in Israel," *Medical Anthropological Quarterly* 17, no. 1 (2003): 78–98, at 86.

35. Ragoné, *Surrogate Motherhood: Conception in the Heart*, 26.

36. Ibid., 79.

37. Ibid., 80.

38. Pande, "Commercial Surrogacy in India," 977.

39. Hochschild, *The Managed Heart: Commercialization of Human Feeling*; A. R. Hochschild, *The Commodification of Intimate Life: Notes from Home and Work* (Berkeley: University of California Press, 2003); Wolkowitz, *Bodies at Work*.

40. Satz, *Why Some Things Should Not Be For Sale*, 131.

41. Richard Titmuss, *The Gift Relationship: From Human Blood to Social Policy* (London: George Allen and Unwin, 1970). For a recent sympathetic account, see David Archard, "Selling Yourself: Titmuss's Argument against a Market in Blood," *Journal of Ethics* 6 (2002): 87–103.

42. Schultz, "Reproductive Technology and Intent-Based Parenthood," 378.

43. Donna Dickenson, *Body Shopping: The Economy Fuelled by Flesh and Blood* (Oxford: OneWorld, 2008), 86.

44. Mary Lyndon Shanley and Sujatha Jesudason, "Surrogacy: Reinscribing or Pluralizing Understandings of Family?" in *Families— Beyond the Nuclear Ideal: For Better or Worse?*, ed. Daniela Cutas and Sarah Chan (London: Bloomsbury Academic, 2012).

Chapter Four

1. Quong, "Left-Libertarianism: Rawlsian not Luck Egalitarian," 64–89, at 87.

2. Lori Andrews and Dorothy Nelkin, *Body Bazaar: The Market for Human Tissue in the Biotechnology Age* (New York: Crown Publishers, 2001), 4.

3. Andrews and Nelkin, *Body Bazaar*, 5.

4. Suzanne Holland, "Contested Commodities at Both Ends of Life: Buying and Selling Gametes, Embryos, and Body Tissues," *Kennedy Institute of Ethics Journal* 11, no. 3 (2001): 263–84, at 261.

5. For material on the United States, and more specifically, the robbing of African American graves, see Michele Goodwin, *Black Markets: The Supply and Demand of Body Parts* (Cambridge: Cambridge University Press, 2006). Burke and Hare operated in Edinburgh, and it seems that what started as the illicit sale of someone who died from natural causes became a series of murders, with victims' bodies then sold to the medical school.

6. Although some remnant of that division of the world remains in the way presumed consent operates in a number of US states. Those who undergo a mandatory autopsy (often, then, the victims of a homicide) are presumed to have consented to the use of their organs unless they explicitly objected prior to their death.

7. Titmuss, *The Gift Relationship*.

8. Fabre, *Whose Body Is It Anyway?*, 137.

9. Lewis Hyde comments on the *lack* of deliberation that characterises decisions to give a kidney to a relative or close friend. Far from going through a careful cost-benefit analysis, many kidney donors report an instantaneous decision, made as soon as they learn of the need. Lewis Hyde, *The Gift* (New York: Random House, 1983), chap. 4.

10. Alireza Baghari, "Compensated Kidney Exchange: A Review of the Iranian Model," *Journal of the Kennedy Institute of Ethics* 16, no. 3 (2006): 269–82.

11. Arguments for this include Richards et al., "The Case for Allowing Kidney Sales," 1950–52; Richards, *The Ethics of Transplants: Why Careless Thought Costs Lives*; Erin and Harris, "A Monopsonistic Market," 134–53; Savulescu "Is the Sale of Body Parts Wrong?," 138–39; James Stacey Taylor, *Stakes and Kidneys: Why Markets in Human Body Parts are Morally Imperative* (Aldershot: Ashgate, 2005).

12. Roger Brownsword, "Property in Human Tissue: Triangulating the Issue," in *Altruism Reconsidered: Exploring New Approaches to Property in Human Tissue*, ed. M. Steinmann, P. Sýkora, and U. Wiesing (Farnham: Ashgate, 2009), 93–104.

13. The full comment is as follows: "I believe we are different from and not identical with our body, at least in the morally relevant sense. Our body is a complex machine that supports our conscious and subconscious life. But it is our mental life which constitutes who we are, not the machine that supports it. I am my mind. My body allows my mind to express itself and shapes who I am, but mind and body are different." J. Savulescu, "Death, Us, and Our Bodies: Personal Reflections," *Journal of Medical Ethics* 29 (2003): 127–30, at 127.

14. Erin and Harris, "A Monopsonistic Market"; John Harris, *Clones, Genes, and Immortality* (Oxford: Oxford University Press, 1998).

15. John Harris, *Enhancing Evolution: The Ethical Case for Making Better People* (Princeton, NJ: Princeton University Press, 2007), 192. He therefore considers mandatory participation ethically defensible but argues against it because it is likely to be more effective to proceed by persuasion.

16. Nancy Scheper-Hughes, "Bodies for Sale—Whole or in Parts," *Body and Society* 7, no. 2–3 (2001): 1–8; and "Commodity Fetishism in Organs Trafficking," 31–62.

17. Radin, *Contested Commodities*, 6.

18. Recompense is used in the recent UK study on *Human Bodies: Donation for Medicine and Research* to cover both reimbursement (direct repayment for financial losses) and compensation (for nonfinancial losses such as discomfort). (London: Nuffield Council on Bioethics, 2011). I discuss their arguments at greater length in chapter five.

19. L. D. de Castro, "Commodification and Exploitation: Arguments in Favour of Compensated Organ Donation," *Journal of Medical Ethics* 29 (2003): 142–46 at 143. See also Fabre, *Whose Body Is It Anyway?*, chap. 6, for a similar argument.

20. Diane M. Tober, "Semen as Gift, Semen as Goods: Reproductive Workers and the Market in Altruism," *Body and Society* 7, no. 2–3 (2001): 137–60, at 150.

21. M. Goyal, R. L. Mehta, L. J. Schniederman, and A. R Sehgal, "Economic and Health Consequences of Selling a Kidney in India," *Journal of the American Medical Association* 288, no. 13 (2002): 1589–93.

22. For example, Wilkinson, *Bodies for Sale*.

23. Ibid., 50.

24. Ibid., 53.

25. Fabre, *Whose Body Is It Anyway?*, 13.

26. Ibid., 14.

27. Donna Dickenson discusses a troubling case of hand transplant in *Body Shopping*, 141–50.

28. Jürgen Habermas makes a similar distinction between having and being in *The Future of Human Nature* (Cambridge: Polity Press, 2003), 50.

29. Radin, *Contested Commodities*.

30. Satz, *Why Some Things Should Not Be For Sale*, 120.

31. Fabre, *Whose Body Is It Anyway?*, 145.

32. In the case of the United Kingdom, for example, this might mean buying from within the European Union. Erin and Harris, "A Monopsonistic Market."

33. Harris himself seems to recognise this in a later contribution, when he describes the regulatory system necessary to protect donors and recipients as "not easy to provide internationally although not of course impossible." Harris, *Enhancing Evolution*, 30.

34. For example, in Arghiri Emmanuel, *Unequal Exchange* (New York and London: Monthly Review Press, 1972).

35. Hyde, *The Gift*, 71.

36. Lawrence Cohen, "Where It Hurts: Indian Material for an Ethics of Organ Transplantation," *Daedalus* 128, no. 4 (1999): 135–65, at 161.

37. Scheper-Hughes, "Commodity Fetishism in Organs Trafficking," 54.

38. Jonathan Beecher and Richard Bienvenu, eds., *The Utopian Vision of Charles Fourier* (London: Jonathan Cape, 1972).

39. Rajeev Bhargava, "Hegel, Taylor, and the Phenomenology of Broken Spirits," in *The Plural States of Recognition*, ed. Michel Seymour (New York: Palgrave Macmillan, 2010), 37–60.

40. Bhargava, "Hegel, Taylor, and the Phenomenology of Broken Spirits," 56.

41. Many of Michele Goodwin's arguments for a market in organs reflect her criticisms of the discriminatory nature of presumed consent. Goodwin, *Black Markets: The Supply and Demand of Body Parts*.

42. The parallel is not, of course, exact. In communal land tenure, one might talk of the land returning to the use of the community on the death of the farmer and his heirs, but one would hardly describe the dead body as "returning" in this way.

43. Fabre, *Whose Body Is It Anyway?*, 99.

44. Andrews and Nelkin, *Body Bazaar*, 7.

45. Ibid., 165.

46. Donna Dickenson, *Women, Property, and Rights* (Cambridge: Polity Press, 1997).

47. Hoppe, *Bioequity: Property and the Human Body*, 4.

48. Critics include Halewood; Andrews and Nelkin, *Body Bazaar*; Dickenson, *Body Shopping*; Nwabueze, *Biotechnology and the Challenge of Property*; Hoppe, *Bioequity: Property and the Human Body*.

49. Hoppe, *Bioequity: Property and the Human Body*, 163.

50. Rebecca Skoot, *The Immortal Life of Henrietta Lacks* (New York: Crown Publishers, 2010).

51. As in the case of Susan Sutton, discussed in Andrews and Nelkin, *Body Bazaar*, 39–40.

52. Holland, "Contested Commodities at Both Ends of Life," 266.

53. As proposed by the Human Genome Organisation (HUGO) Ethics Committee in 2000. See the discussion in Caroline Mullen and Heather Widdows, "An Investigation of the Conception, Management, and Regulation of Tangible and Intangible Property in Human Tissues: The PropEur Project," in Steinmann, Sýkora, and Weising, *Altruism Reconsidered: Exploring New Approaches to Property in Human Tissue*, 169–81.

54. Holland, "Contested Commodities at Both Ends of Life," 263–64.

55. *The Washington University v. Dr. W. Catalona et al.* (March 31, 2006).

56. For a balanced discussion of the case see Dickenson, *Body Shopping*, 117–31.

57. *Greenberg and others v. Miami Children's Hospital Research Institute* 264 F Supp 2d 1064 (2003).

58. Andrews and Nelkin, *Body Bazaar*, 161.

59. *Regina v. Kelly and Lindsay* (C.A.) [1998] 3 All E.R. 741.

60. Discussed in Remigius Nwabueze, "Donated Organs, Property Rights, and the Remedial Quagmire," *Medical Law Review* 16 (2008): 201–24.

61. *Yearworth & Others v. North Bristol NHS Trust* (CA) [2009] EWCA Civ 37.

62. Hoppe, *Property and the Human Body*, 114.

63. Cohen, *Self-Ownership, Freedom, and Equality*, 214.

64. Honoré, "Ownership" in Guest, *Oxford Essays in Jurisprudence*.

65. Anne Phillips, *The Enigma of Colonialism* (London: James Currey, 1991), chap. 2.

66. *Yearworth*, 127.

67. Honoré is invoked, among others, by Brownsword, Hoppe, Dickenson, and Nwabueze.

68. E. Richard Gold, *Body Parts: Property Rights and the Ownership of Human Biological Materials* (Washington, DC: Georgetown University Press, 1997), 173.

69. Consider the related problem in discourses regarding multiculturalism. Nearly all theorists of multiculturalism now endorse a complex and nuanced understanding of culture that recognises the permeability of cultural boundaries, the contestations that take place within each cultural community over what constitutes its core practices, and the fluidity of cultures over time. Yet when the notion of culture is invoked in popular and political discourse, it continues to assume the frozen solidity that these accounts now try to repudiate. See Anne Phillips, *Gender and Culture* (Cambridge: Polity Press, 2010).

70. Petchesky, "The Body as Property: A Feminist Re-Vision," 389.

71. Nedelsky, "Property in Potential Life?," 353n.

Chapter Five

1. Jean Jacques Rousseau, *Discourse on the Origin and Basis of Inequality among Men* (1754). Everyman's Library edition, translated with an introduction by G.D.H. Cole (London: Dent, 1966), 192.

2. Dickenson, *Property, Women, and Politics*, 157.

3. Nuffield Council on Bioethics, *Human Bodies: Donation for Medicine and Research* (London, 2011), 9.

4. Satz, *Why Some Things Should Not Be For Sale*, 147.

5. Ibid., 129.

6. Ibid., 131.

7. Widdows, "Rejecting the Choice Paradigm," in Madhok, Phillips, and Wilson, *Gender, Agency, and Coercion*.

8. Richards et al., "The Case for Allowing Kidney Sales," 1950.

9. Satz, *Why Some Things Should Not Be For Sale*, 200.

10. At http://news.discovery.com/human/first-artificial-organ-transplant-110708.html.

11. Heather Widdows, "Border Disputes across Bodies: Exploitation in Trafficking for Prostitution and Egg Sale for Stem Cell

Research," *International Journal of the Feminist Association of Bioethics* 2, no. 1 (2009): 5–24, at 12.

12. Ingrid Schneider, "Indirect Commodification of Ova Donation for Assisted Reproduction and for Human Cloning Research: Proposals for Supranational Regulation," in Steinmann, Sýkora, and Wiesing, *Altruism Reconsidered*, 209–42, at 216.

13. Nuffield Council on Bioethics, *Human Bodies*, 70.

14. Ibid., 181.

15. Avi Katz, "Surrogate Motherhood and the Baby-Selling Laws," *Columbia Journal of Law and Social Problems* 20, no. 1 (1983): 1–54.

16. I owe this example to Emily Jackson.

17. Emily Jackson, "Compensating Egg Donors" in Madhok, Phillips, and Wilson, *Gender, Agency, and Coercion.*

18. At http://www.futurepundit.com/archives/007052.html.

19. Scheper-Hughes "Commodity Fetishism in Organ Trafficking," 49.

20. Pateman, "Self-Ownership and Property in the Person," 51.

Bibliography

Anderson, Elizabeth S. "Is Women's Labor a Commodity?" *Philosophy and Public Affairs* 19, no. 1 (1990): 71–92.

Andrews, Lori B. "Surrogate Motherhood: The Challenge for Feminists." In *The Ethics of Reproductive Technology*, edited by Kenneth D Alpern, 205–19. New York and Oxford: Oxford University Press, 1992.

Andrews, Lori B., and Dorothy Nelkin. *Body Bazaar: The Market for Human Tissue in the Biotechnology Age*. New York: Crown Publishers, 2001.

Andrijasevic, Rutvica. *Migration, Agency, and Citizenship in Sex Trafficking*. New York: Palgrave Macmillan, 2010.

Archard, David. "Selling Yourself: Titmuss's Argument against a Market in Blood." *Journal of Ethics* 6 (2002): 87–103.

———. "The Wrong of Rape." *Philosophical Quarterly* 57, no. 228 (2007): 374–93.

Baber, H. E. "How Bad Is Rape?" *Hypatia* 2, no. 2 (1987): 125–38.

Baghari, Alireza. "Compensated Kidney Exchange: A Review of the Iranian Model." *Journal of the Kennedy Institute of Ethics* 16, no. 3 (2006): 269–82.

Beecher, Jonathan, and Richard Bienvenu, eds. *The Utopian Vision of Charles Fourier*. London: Jonathan Cape, 1972.

Bhargava, Rajeev. "Hegel, Taylor, and the Phenomenology of Broken Spirits." In *The Plural States of Recognition*, edited by Michel Seymour, 37–60. New York: Palgrave Macmillan, 2010.

Björkman, B., and S. O. Hansson. "Bodily Rights and Property Rights." *Journal of Medical Ethics* 32, no. 4 (2006): 209–14.

Bourke, Joanna. *Rape: A History from 1860 to the Present Day*. London: Virago, 2007.

———. *What It Means to Be Human*. New York: Little, Brown, 2011.

Brace, Laura. *The Politics of Property: Labour, Freedom, and Belonging*. Edinburgh: Edinburgh University Press, 2004.

Braverman, Harry, *Labor and Monopoly Capital: The Degradation of Work in the Twentieth Century*. New York and London: Monthly Review Press, 1974.

Brazier, Margaret, Alastair Campbell, and Susan Golombok. *Surrogacy: Review for Health Ministers of Current Arrangements for Payments and Regulation*. London: HMSO, 1998.

Brison, Susan J. *Aftermath: Violence and the Remaking of a Self*. Princeton, NJ: Princeton University Press, 2003.

———. "Outliving Oneself: Trauma, Memory, and Personal Identity." In *Feminists Rethink the Self*, edited by Diana Tietjen Meyers, 12–39. Boulder, CO: Westview Press, 1997.

Brownmiller, Susan. *Against Our Will: Men, Women, and Rape*. New York: Simon and Schuster, 1975.

Brownsword, Roger. "Property in Human Tissue: Triangulating the Issue." In *Altruism Reconsidered: Exploring New Approaches to Property in Human Tissue*, edited by M. Steinmann, P. Sýkora, and U. Wiesing, 93–104. Farnham: Ashgate, 2009.

Busby, Karen, and Delaney Vun. "Revisiting The Handmaid's Tale: Feminist Theory Meets Empirical Research on Surrogate Mothers." *Canadian Journal of Family Law* 26, no. 1 (2010): 13–94.

Butler, Judith. *Frames of War: When Is Life Grievable?* London: Verso, 2009.

Cahill, Ann J. *Rethinking Rape*. Ithaca, NY: Cornell University Press, 2001.

Castro, L. D., de. "Commodification and Exploitation: Arguments in Favour of Compensated Organ Donation." *Journal of Medical Ethics* 29 (2003): 142–46.

Christman, John. *The Myth of Property: Toward an Egalitarian Theory of Ownership*. New York and Oxford: Oxford University Press, 1994.

Clark, Lorenne M. G., and Debra J. Lewis. *Rape: The Price of Coercive Sexuality*. Toronto: The Women's Press, 1977.

Cochrane, Alasdair. "Ownership and Justice for Animals." *Utilitas* 21, no. 4 (2009): 424–42.

Cohen, G. A. *Self-Ownership, Freedom, and Equality*. Cambridge: Cambridge University Press, 1995.

Cohen, Lawrence. "Where It Hurts: Indian Material for an Ethics of Organ Transplantation." *Daedalus* 128, no. 4 (1990): 135–65.

Coleman, Janet. "Pre-Modern Property and Self-Ownership before and after Locke; or, When Did Common Decency Become a Private Rather Than a Public Virtue?" *European Journal of Political Theory* 4, no. 2 (2005): 125–45.

Corea, Gena. *The Mother Machine: Reproductive Technologies from Artificial Insemination to Artificial Wombs*. New York: Harper and Row, 1985.

Davis, Michael. "Setting Penalties: What Does Rape Deserve?" *Law and Philosophy* 3, no. 1 (1984): 61–110.

Dickenson, Donna. *Body Shopping: The Economy Fuelled by Flesh and Blood*. Oxford: OneWorld, 2008.

———. *Property in the Body: Feminist Perspectives*. Cambridge: Cambridge University Press, 2007.

———. *Property, Women, and Politics*. Cambridge: Polity Press, 1997.

Donchin, Anne. "Feminist Critiques of New Fertility Technologies: Implications for Social Policy." *Journal of Medicine and Philosophy* 21 (1996): 475–98.

Dripps, Donald A. "Beyond Rape: An Essay on the Difference between the Presence of Force and the Absence of Consent." *Columbia Law Review* 92 (1992): 1780–809.

Du Toit, Louise. *A Philosophical Investigation of Rape: The Making and Unmaking of the Feminine Self*. New York and London: Routledge, 2009.

Dworkin, Ronald. "Comment on Narveson: In Defence of Equality." *Social Philosophy and Policy* 1 (1983): 24–40.

Emmanuel, Arghiri. *Unequal Exchange*. New York and London: Monthly Review Press, 1972.

Erin, Charles A., and John Harris. "A Monopsonistic Market: Or How to Buy and Sell Human Organs, Tissues, and Cells Ethically." In *Life and Death under High Technology Medicine*, edited by Ian Robinson, 134–53. Manchester: Manchester University Press, 1994.

Ertman, Martha M., and Joan C. Williams, eds. *Rethinking Commodification: Cases and Readings in Law and Culture*. New York: New York University Press, 2005.

Eyal, Nir. "Is the Body Special?" *Utilitas* 21, no. 2 (2009): 233–45.

Fabre, Cécile. *Whose Body Is It Anyway?* New York: Oxford University Press, 2006.

Folbre, Nancy. *The Invisible Heart: Economics and Family Values*. New York: New Press, 2001.

———. *Who Pays for the Kids? Gender and the Structures of Constraint*. London and New York: Routledge, 1996.

Gatens, Moira. *Imaginary Bodies: Ethics, Power, and Corporeality*. London: Routledge, 1996.

Gold, Richard. *Body Parts: Property Rights and the Ownership of Human Biological Materials.* Washington, DC: Georgetown University Press, 1997.

Goodwin, Michele. *Black Markets: The Supply and Demand of Body Parts.* Cambridge: Cambridge University Press, 2006.

Goyal, M., R. L. Mehta, L. J. Schniederman, and A. R. Sehgal. "Economic and Health Consequences of Selling a Kidney in India." *Journal of the American Medical Association* 288, no. 13 (2002): 1589–93.

Grosz, Elizabeth. *Volatile Bodies.* Bloomington: Indiana University Press, 1994.

Habermas, Jürgen. *The Future of Human Nature.* Cambridge: Polity Press, 2003.

Halewood, Peter. "On Commodification and Self-Ownership." *Yale Journal of Law and the Humanities* 20 (2008): 131–62.

Hall, Rachel. "'It Can Happen to You': Rape Prevention in the Age of Risk Management." *Hypatia* 19, no. 3 (2004): 1–19.

Hampton, Jean. "Defining Wrong and Defining Rape." In *A Most Detestable Crime: New Philosophical Essays on Rape,* edited by Keith Burgess-Jackson, 118–58. New York and Oxford: Oxford University Press, 1999.

Harris, J. W. "Who Owns My Body?" *Oxford Journal of Legal Studies* 16, no. 1 (1996): 55–84.

Harris, John. *Clones, Genes, and Immortality.* Oxford: Oxford University Press, 1998.

———. *Enhancing Evolution: The Ethical Case for Making Better People.* Princeton, NJ: Princeton University Press, 2007.

Hochschild, Arlie Russell. *The Commodification of Intimate Life: Notes from Home and Work.* Berkeley: University of California Press, 2003.

———. *The Managed Heart: Commercialization of Human Feeling.* Berkeley: University of California Press, 1983.

Hohfeld, Wesley Newcomb. "Fundamental Legal Conceptions as Applied in Judicial Reasoning." *Yale Law Journal* 26, no. 8 (1917): 710–70.

Holland, Suzanne. "Contested Commodities at Both Ends of Life: Buying and Selling Gametes, Embryos, and Body Tissues." *Kennedy Institute of Ethics Journal* 11, no. 3 (2001): 263–84.

Honoré, A. M. "Ownership." In *Oxford Essays in Jurisprudence,* edited by A. G. Guest. Oxford: Oxford University Press, 1961.

Hoppe, Nils. *Bioequity: Property and the Human Body*. Aldershot: Ashgate, 2009.

Hunt, Lynn. *Inventing Human Rights*. New York: W. W. Norton, 2007.

Hyde, Lewis. *The Gift*. New York: Random House, 1983.

Ikemoto, Lisa C. "Eggs as Capital: Human Egg Procurement in the Fertility Industry and the Stem Cell Research Enterprise." *Signs* 34, no. 4 (2009): 763–81.

———. "Reproductive Tourism: Equality Concerns in the Global Market for Fertility Services." *Law and Inequality* 27 (2009): 277–309.

Jackson, Emily. "Compensating Egg Donors." In *Gender, Agency, and Coercion*, edited by Sumi Madhok, Anne Phillips, and Kalpana Wilson, 181–94. Basingstoke: Palgrave Macmillan, 2013.

Kant, Immanuel. *Lectures on Ethics*. Cambridge: Cambridge University Press, 1992.

Katz, Avi. "Surrogate Motherhood and the Baby-Selling Laws." *Columbia Journal of Law and Social Problems* 20, no. 1 (1983): 1–54.

Kritzman, Lawrence D., ed. *Politics, Philosophy, Culture: Interviews and Other Writings, 1972–1984*, by Michel Foucault. New York and London: Routledge, 1988.

Kruks, Sonia. *Retrieving Experience*. Ithaca, NY: Cornell University Press, 2001.

Lacey, Nicola. "Unspeakable Subjects, Impossible Rights: Sexuality, Integrity, and Criminal Law." *Canadian Journal of Law and Jurisprudence* 11, no. 1 (1998): 47–68.

Landes, E. M., and R. A. Posner. "The Economics of the Baby Shortage." *Journal of Legal Studies* 7 (June 1978): 323–48.

Larson, Jane E. "Women Understand So Little, They Call My Good Nature 'Deceit': A Feminist Rethinking of Seduction." *Columbia Law Review* 93, no. 2 (1993): 375–472.

Laufer-Ukeles, Pamela. "Gestation: Work for Hire or the Essence of Motherhood? A Comparative Legal Analysis." *Duke Journal of Gender Law and Policy* 9 (2002): 91–134.

Lloyd, Genevieve. *The Man of Reason: "Male" and "Female" in Western Philosophy*. London: Methuen, 1986.

Locke, John. *Second Treatise on Government*, 1690.

Lukács, Georg. *History and Class Consciousness*. 1922; London: Merlin Press, 1968.

MacKinnon, Catharine A. "Prostitution and Civil Rights." *Michigan Journal of Gender and Law* 1 (1993): 13–31.

MacKinnon, Catharine A. *Toward a Feminist Theory of the State*. Cambridge, MA: Harvard University Press, 1989.

Macpherson, C. B. *The Political Theory of Possessive Individualism*. Oxford: Clarendon Press, 1962.

Madhok, Sumi, Anne Phillips, and Kalpana Wilson, eds. *Gender, Agency, and Coercion*. Basingstoke: Palgrave Macmillan, 2013.

Marcus, Sharon. "Fighting Bodies, Fighting Words: A Theory and Politics of Rape Prevention." In *Feminists Theorize the Political*, edited by Judith Butler and Joan W. Scott, 385–403. New York and London: Routledge, 1992.

Mardorossian, Carine M. "Toward a New Feminist Theory of Rape." *Signs* 27, no. 3 (2002): 743–75.

McGregor, Joan. "Force, Consent, and the Reasonable Woman." In *In Harm's Way: Essays in Honor of Joel Feinberg*, edited by Jules L. Coleman and Allen Buchanan, 231–54. Cambridge: Cambridge University Press, 1994.

———. *Is It Rape? On Acquaintance Rape and Taking Women's Consent Seriously*. Aldershot: Ashgate, 2005.

Miriam, Kathy. "Stopping the Traffic in Women: Power, Agency, and Abolition in Feminist Debates over Sex Trafficking." *Journal of Social Philosophy* 36, no. 1 (2005): 1–17.

Moi, Toril. *What Is a Woman? And Other Essays*. Oxford: Oxford University Press, 1999.

Moyn, Samuel. *The Last Utopia: Human Rights in History*. Cambridge, MA: Harvard University Press, 2010.

Mullen, Caroline, and Heather Widdows. "An Investigation of the Conception, Management, and Regulation of Tangible and Intangible Property in Human Tissues: The PropEur Project." In *Altruism Reconsidered: Exploring New Approaches to Property in Human Tissue*, edited by M. Steinmann, P. Sýkora, and U. Wiesing, 169–82. Farnham: Ashgate, 2009.

Murphy, Jeffrie G. "Some Ruminations on Women, Violence, and the Criminal Law." In *In Harm's Way: Essays in Honor of Joel Feinberg*, edited by Jules L. Coleman and Allen Buchanan, 209–30. Cambridge: Cambridge University Press, 1994.

Naffine, Ngaire. "The Legal Status of Self-Ownership: Or the Self-Possessed Man and the Woman Possessed." *Journal of Law and Society* 25, no. 2 (1988): 193–212.

Narayan, Uma. "The 'Gift' of a Child: Commercial Surrogacy, Gift Surrogacy, and Motherhood." In *Expecting Trouble: Surrogacy, Fetal Abuse, and New Reproductive Technologies*, edited by Patricia Boling, 177–201. Boulder, CO: Westview Press, 1995.

Nedelsky, Jennifer. "Are Persons Property?" *Adelaide Law Review* 24 (2003): 123–31.

———. "Boundaries and the Bounded Self." *Representations* 30 (1990): 162–89.

———. "Property in Potential Life? A Relational Approach to Choosing Legal Categories." *Canadian Journal of Law and Jurisprudence* 6, no. 2 (1993): 343–66.

———. "Reconceiving Autonomy." *Yale Journal of Law and Feminism* 1 (1989): 7–36.

———. "Violence against Women: Challenges to the Liberal State and Relational Feminism." In *Political Order*, edited by Ian Shapiro and Russell Hardin, 454–97. Nomos 38. New York: New York University Press, 1995.

Nozick, Robert. *Anarchy, State, and Utopia*. New York: Harper and Row, 1974.

Nuffield Council on Bioethics. *Human Bodies: Donation for Medicine and Research*. London, 2011.

Nussbaum, Martha C. "Objectification." *Philosophy and Public Affairs* 24, no. 4 (1995): 249–91.

———. " 'Whether from Reason or Prejudice': Taking Money for Bodily Services." In *Sex and Social Justice*. New York: Oxford University Press, 1999.

Nwabueze, Remigius. *Biotechnology and the Challenge of Property: Property Rights In Dead Bodies, Body Parts, and Genetic Information*. Aldershot: Ashgate, 2007.

———. "Donated Organs, Property Rights, and the Remedial Quagmire." *Medical Law Review* 16 (2008): 201–24.

O'Connell Davidson, Julia. "The Rights and Wrongs of Prostitution." *Hypatia* 17, no. 2 (2002): 84–98.

Overall, Christine. *Human Reproduction: Principles, Practices, Policies*. Toronto and Oxford: Oxford University Press, 1993.

———. " 'Pluck a Fetus from Its Womb': A Critique of Current Attitudes toward the Embryo/Fetus." *University of Western Ontario Law Review* 24 (1986–87): 1–14.

Paglia, Camille. *Sex, Art, and American Culture.* New York: Vintage, 1992.

Pande, Amrita. "'At Least I Am Not Sleeping with Anyone': Resisting the Stigma of Commercial Surrogacy in India." *Feminist Studies* 36, no. 2 (2010): 292–312.

——. "Commercial Surrogacy in India: Manufacturing a Perfect Mother-Worker." *Signs* 35, no. 4 (2010): 969–92.

Pateman, Carole. "Self-Ownership and Property in the Person." *Journal of Political Philosophy* 10 (2002): 20–53.

——. *The Sexual Contract.* Cambridge: Polity Press, 1988.

Pettit, Philip. *Republicanism: A Theory of Freedom and Government.* Oxford: Oxford University Press, 1999.

Phillips, Anne. *The Enigma of Colonialism.* London: James Currey, 1991.

——. *Gender and Culture.* Cambridge: Polity Press, 2010.

——. *The Politics of Presence.* Oxford: Oxford University Press, 1995.

Phoenix, Joanna. *Making Sense of Prostitution.* New York: St. Martin's Press, 1999.

Plaza, Monique. "Our Damages and Their Compensation, Rape: The Will Not to Know of Michel Foucault." *Feminist Issues* 1, no. 2 (1981): 29. French edition 1978.

Pollack Petchesky, Rosalind. "The Body as Property: A Feminist Re-Vision." In *Conceiving the New World Order: The Global Politics of Reproduction*, edited by Faye D. Ginsburg and Rayna Rapp, 387–406. Berkeley: University of California Press, 1995.

Posner, Richard A. "The Ethics of Enforcing Contracts of Surrogate Motherhood." *Journal of Contemporary Health Law and Policy* 5 (1989): 21–31.

——. *Sex and Reason.* Cambridge, MA: Harvard University Press, 1992.

Prokhovnik, Raia. *Rational Woman: A Feminist Critique of Dichotomy.* London: Routledge, 1999.

Purdy, Laura M. *Reproducing Persons: Issues in Feminist Bioethics.* Ithaca, NY: Cornell University Press, 1996.

Puwar, Nirmal. *Space Invaders: Race, Gender, and Bodies Out of Place.* Oxford: Berg, 2004.

Quong, Jonathan. "Left-Libertarianism: Rawlsian not Luck Egalitarian." *Journal of Political Philosophy* 19, no. 1 (2011): 64–89.

Radin, Margaret Jane. *Contested Commodities: The Trouble with Trade in Sex, Children, Body Parts, and Other Things*. Cambridge, MA: Harvard University Press, 1996.

Ragoné, Helena. *Surrogate Motherhood: Conception in the Heart*. Boulder, CO: Westview Press, 1994.

Richards, Janet Radcliffe. *The Ethics of Transplants: Why Careless Thought Costs Lives*. Oxford: Oxford University Press, 2012.

Richards, Janet Radcliffe, A. S. Daar, R. D. Guttmann, R. Hoffenberg, I. Kennedy, M. Lock, R. A. Sells, and N. Tilney. "The Case for Allowing Kidney Sales." *The Lancet* 351, no. 9120 (1998): 1950–52.

Roiphe, Katie. *The Morning After: Sex, Fear, and Feminism on Campus*. Boston: Little, Brown, 1993.

Rose, Carol M. *Property and Persuasion: Essays on the History, Theory, and Rhetoric of Ownership*. Boulder, CO: Westview Press, 1994.

———. "Whither Commodification?" In *Rethinking Commodification: Cases and Readings in Law and Culture*, edited by Martha M. Ertman and Joan C. Williams, 402–27. New York: New York University Press, 2005.

Rousseau, Jean-Jacques. *Discourse on the Origin and Basis of Inequality among Men* (1754). Everyman's Library edition, translated with an introduction by G.D.H. Cole. London: Dent, 1966.

Sandel, Michael J. *The Case against Perfectionism*. Cambridge, MA: Belknap Press of Harvard University Press, 2007.

———. *What Money Can't Buy: The Moral Limits of Markets*. New York and London: Allen Lane, 2012.

Satz, Debra. "Markets in Women's Sexual Labor." *Ethics* 106 (1995): 63–85.

———. *Why Some Things Should Not Be For Sale: The Moral Limits of Markets*. Oxford and New York: Oxford University Press, 2010.

Savulescu, Julian. "Death, Us, and Our Bodies: Personal Reflections." *Journal of Medical Ethics* 29 (2003): 127–30.

———. "Is the Sale of Body Parts Wrong?" *Journal of Medical Ethics* 29 (2003): 138–39.

Scheper-Hughes, Nancy. "Bodies for Sale—Whole or in Parts." *Body and Society* 7, no. 2–3 (2001): 1–8.

———. "Commodity Fetishism in Organs Trafficking." *Body and Society* 7, no. 2–3 (2001): 31–62.

Schneider, Ingrid. "Indirect Commodification of Ova Donation for Assisted Reproduction and for Human Cloning Research: Proposals for

Supranational Regulation." In *Altruism Reconsidered: Exploring New Approaches to Property in Human Tissue*, edited by Michael Steinmann, Peter Sýkora, and Urban Wiesing, 209–42. Farnham: Ashgate, 2009.

Schultz, Marjorie Maguire. "Reproductive Technology and Intent-Based Parenthood: An Opportunity for Gender Neutrality." *Wisconsin Law Review* (1990): 297–398.

Scott, Elizabeth S. "Surrogacy and the Politics of Commodification." *Law and Contemporary Problems* 72 (Summer 2009): 109–46.

Shalev, Carmel. *Birth Power: The Case for Surrogacy*. New Haven, CT: Yale University Press, 1989.

Shanley, Mary Lyndon. "'Surrogate Mothering' and Women's Freedom: A Critique of Contracts for Human Reproduction." *Signs* 18 (1993): 618–39.

Shanley, Mary Lyndon, and Sujatha Jesudason. "Surrogacy: Reinscribing or Pluralizing Understandings of Family?" In *Families—Beyond the Nuclear Ideal: For Better or Worse?*, edited by Daniela Cutas and Sarah Chan. London: Bloomsbury Academic, 2012.

Shildrick, Margrit. *Leaky Bodies and Boundaries: Feminism, Postmodernism, and (Bio)ethics*. New York and London: Routledge, 1997.

Silbaugh, Katherine. "Commodification and Women's Household Labor." In *Rethinking Commodification: Cases and Readings in Law and Culture*, edited by Martha M. Ertman, and Joan C. Williams, 297–302. New York: New York University Press, 2005.

Skoot, Rebecca. *The Immortal Life of Henrietta Lacks*. New York: Crown Publishers, 2010.

Taylor, James Stacey. *Stakes and Kidneys: Why Markets in Human Body Parts are Morally Imperative*. Aldershot: Ashgate, 2005.

Teman, Elly. "The Medicalization of 'Nature' in the 'Artificial Body': Surrogate Motherhood in Israel." *Medical Anthropological Quarterly* 17, no. 1 (2003): 78–98.

Titmuss, Richard M. *The Gift Relationship: From Human Blood to Social Policy*. London: George Allen and Unwin, 1970.

Tober, Diane M. "Semen as Gift, Semen as Goods: Reproductive Workers and the Market in Altruism." *Body and Society* 7, no. 2–3 (2001): 137–60.

Vallentyne, Peter, and Hillel Steiner, eds. *Left-Libertarianism and Its Critics: The Contemporary Debate*. New York: Palgrave, 2000.

———. *The Origins of Left-Libertarianism: An Anthology of Historical Writings.* New York: Palgrave, 2000.

Waldron, Jeremy. *The Right to Private Property.* Oxford: Clarendon Press, 1988.

Wald, Alexandra. "What's Rightfully Ours: Toward a Property Theory of Rape." *Columbia Journal of Law and Social Problems* 30 (1996–97): 459–502.

Wertheimer, Alan. *Consent to Sexual Relations.* Cambridge: Cambridge University Press, 2003.

West, Robin. "Legitimating the Illegitimate: A Comment on 'Beyond Rape.'" *Columbia Law Review* 93 (1993): 1442–59.

Widdows, Heather. "Border Disputes across Bodies: Exploitation in Trafficking for Prostitution and Egg Sale for Stem Cell Research." *International Journal of the Feminist Association of Bioethics* 2, no. 1 (2009): 5–24.

———. "Rejecting the Choice Paradigm: Rethinking the Ethical Framework in Prostitution and Egg Sale Debates." In *Gender, Agency, and Coercion,* edited by Sumi Madhok, Anne Phillips, and Kalpana Wilson, 157–80. Basingstoke: Palgrave Macmillan, 2013.

Wilkinson, Stephen. *Bodies for Sale: Ethics and Exploitation in the Human Body Trade.* London: Routledge, 2003.

Young, Iris M. *On Female Body Experience: Throwing Like a Girl and Other Essays.* Oxford: Oxford University Press, 2005.

Index

abduction, 42, 43
abortion, 21, 83, 102
Abraham and Sarah and Hagar, 67
adoption, 75, 77, 85, 86, 92, 95
agency: and body parts market, 8, 113; and choice, 8–9; and degree of voluntariness, 9; and labour safety requirements, 90–91; and payment, 150; and property, 32; and prostitution and surrogacy, 70; and self-ownership, 19–20; and sex workers, 6; of surrogates, 76–80, 85; and thing-like status, 19–20; of women, 79
alienation: and Dickenson, 37; and labour as property, 37; and Marxism, 5; and self-ownership, 129; and surrogacy, 82, 85, 87. *See also* self-alienation
altruism, 138, 139, 142, 143. *See also* surrogacy, altruistic
American Society for Reproductive Medicine, 150
Anderson, Elizabeth, 74, 81–82, 87
Andrews, Lori, 98, 123, 128
Andrijasevic, Rutvica, 70
Archard, David, 49, 52, 58, 166n18
artificial insemination, 67. *See also* sperm
assault, 15, 48, 50, 51, 52, 59
Australia, 91–92
autonomy, 18, 48; and constructive relationships, 55; denial of, 23, 24; exclusionary and protective understanding of, 55; loss of, 10; and property, 22, 55
autopsy, 120, 172n6

Baber, Harriet, 52–53
Baby M case, 68–69, 77–78, 79, 84, 141

beauty contests, 24
beauty industry, 18
Beauvoir, Simone de, *The Second Sex*, 18, 29
Bhangis, 119
Bhargava, Rajeev, 119
biotechnology, 13, 33–34, 124, 134. *See also* medical technology; reproductive technology
blood, 33–34, 98, 99, 105
blood donation: compensation for, 101; demands of, 101, 102; and payment, 93, 99–100, 138; and reciprocity, 102; and surrogacy, 101–2; and *Washington University v. Dr. W. Catalona et al.*, 127, 132
bodily integrity, 15, 136; and body or self as property, 21; and human rights, 37–38; and pain, 37–38; and rape, 45, 46, 52, 54–55; relationship and reciprocity in, 56; right to, 19; and self-ownership, 38; and self-possession, 38; and territorial integrity, 57
bodily services, 28; and body as property, 65–66, 123–24, 131, 137–38, 142–43; and body ownership, 152; commercialisation of, 153; and embodied experience of labour, 10; and embodied self, 30; and feminism, 27; and individual vs. society, 137–38; and labour contracts, 82–83; market in, 6, 9, 16, 26, 27, 30, 65, 137–38; payment vs. compensation for, 108; and prohibition on touch, 31; and property language, 123–24; and rental of body, 69; and risks of body property, 15; sale of, 28; and self-ownership, 26

wealth of buyers of, 114. *See also* eggs; organ donation

body parts, market in, 2, 16; and agency, 8, 113; bans on, 145; and benefits to those in need, 105; coercion in, 6–7; and commodification, 123; compensation for, 101; and consent, 7, 120–21; contingent vs. essential features of, 113; and economic necessity, 114; and embodied self, 30; and equality, 11, 113, 153; and feminism, 27; and fungibility, 25; and human inequality, 140; and individual vs. society, 137–38; and mind/body dualisms, 29; motivations of recipients in, 117; and poor people, 7, 113, 114; and property, 122–33; and property rights, 105; and self-ownership, 26, 123; and sense of self, 105; and specialisation, 115, 120; utilitarian perspective on, 105; and vulnerability, 113

boundaries and boundary crossing, 45, 54–57, 167n35

boundary integrity, 23

Bourke, Joanna, 38–39, 61

Brison, Susan, 56, 62–63

Brownmiller, Susan, *Against Our Will*, 42, 52

Brownsword, Roger, 104–5, 106

Burke and Hare murders, 99, 172n5

Butler, Judith, 38

Canada, 91–92; Assisted Human Reproduction Act, 92

capacities, 27, 35–37

capitalism, 22, 32

Castro, L. D., de, 108–9

Catholic Church, 3

childbearing, 28, 101, 102

child labour, 90, 144, 145, 146

children/babies: adopted, 86; best interests of, 76, 77, 78, 93; and body or self as property, 21; commodification of, 72–76, 96; equally

shared care for, 81; as extension of parents, 75–76; identity problems for, 70–71; knowledge of surrogates and gamete providers for, 95–96; markets in, 2; relinquishment of, 67, 84–91; sexual relations with adults, 166–67n26; as things bought and sold, 72–76. *See also* adoption; surrogacy

China, 103

choice, 152; and agency, 8–9; and banning markets, 143, 144, 146; and individuals, 138, 139, 142, 143; in labour, 90–91; and markets, 7; and property, 131; and prostitution, 8, 70; of surrogates, 70, 97. *See also* coercion; consent

Clark, Lorenne, 43–44, 52

coercion, 6, 7, 47, 150

Cohen, G. A., 40–41, 129, 162n29, 164n58

Cohen, Lawrence, 117

Colavito v. New York Organ Donor Network, 128–29

commercialisation, 5, 71, 100, 105, 152, 153

commissioning parents, 31, 67, 101; and adoption, 75; awareness of surrogate's health and welfare, 110; as changing minds, 85; and child as commodity, 74–75; and child's knowledge of surrogates, 96; and choice of surrogacy, 74–75; compensation from, 94; and contract, 76–77; cost to, 68; in Israel, 68, 77; and property and contract rights, 35; relationship with surrogate, 88–89. *See also* surrogacy; surrogates

commodification, 1, 123, 153, 159n21; of babies, 72–76, 96; of bodies, 5, 13, 22–23, 41; of body parts, 108; and body parts market, 123; and commercial surrogacy, 70; defined, 25–26; and exploitation, 104, 106; and feminism, 13, 27; of kidney

119; and surrogacy, 12, 140; and voluntary trade in body, 12; of women and men, 14
Erin, Charles, 114
Europe, 68
Eyal, Nir, 1

Fabre, Cécile, 100, 103, 111, 113–14, 121–22, 123, 162n30
feminism, 1, 22; and abortion, 102; and bodily services market, 27; and body, 27–31; and body as owned, 5; and body parts market, 27; and commercial surrogacy, 28, 77, 78–79; and commodification, 13, 27; and desexualisation of rape, 52–53; and eggs, 27; and mind/body dualism, 27, 29; and objectification, 18, 27; and prostitution, 27, 28; and rape, 44, 52–53; and reason vs. emotion, 29; and reproductive technology, 71; and self-propriety, 20; and surrogacy, 27, 71
fertility/infertility, 3, 4, 75, 89, 92, 101, 102, 105, 109, 151, 153–54
Florida, 77
football, 10, 30
Foucault, Michel, 50, 52, 166–67n26
Fourier, Charles, 118–19
fungibility, 23, 25, 112

gametes, 2, 4; child's knowledge of providers of, 95–96; compensation for, 103; donor, 98; markets in, 147–48; payment for, 150–51; purchase price for, 149; as shared resource, 134. *See also* eggs; embryos
gay couples, 70
Georgia, 67
gifts/gift relationships, 93, 100, 101, 116–17
Gold, Richard, 131
Goodwin, Michele, 174n41
Greenberg, Dan, 127

Greenberg, Debbie, 127
Greenberg v. Miami Children's Hospital, 127
grief, 38

Halewood, Peter, 26–27
Hall, Rachel, 63
Hampton, Jean, 59–60
Harris, John, 105, 114, 122–23, 132, 173n15, 174n33
Harris, J. W., 15, 21, 41
Hegel, G.W.F., 32
Hochschild, Arlie, 90; *The Managed Heart*, 5
Hohfeld, Wesley Newcomb, 32
Holland, Suzanne, 98, 125, 127, 132
Honoré, A. M., 32, 129–30, 131
Hoppe, Nils, 124, 129
human flourishing, 58, 113, 121, 138
Human Genome Organisation (HUGO), 126, 175n53
human rights, 20, 37–38, 99, 136, 163–64n49
Hunt, Lynn, *Inventing Human Rights*, 37–38, 163–64n49
Hyde, Lewis, 116, 172n9

identity: and body, 27, 112, 113, 120; and children of surrogates, 70–71; and commodification, 112, 113, 120; and culture, 167n43; and intrusions into body, 31; and rape, 53, 54, 61, 62; and reproduction, 9; and sexuality, 9, 27, 58; and surrogacy, 91, 94, 95; and surrogacy contracts, 81. *See also* self: sense of
Ikemoto, Lisa, 15, 87–88
Illich, Ivan, 153
India, 66, 67–68, 69–70, 91; caste system of, 119; kidney market in, 109; motivations of body parts recipients in, 117; poverty in, 87–88; and surrogacy contracts, 83–84; surrogacy hostels in, 12; surrogacy in, 77, 168–69n2; surrogates as vessels

India (cont'd)
in, 89; Transplantation of Human
Organs Act of 1994, 103
individual/individualism, 16, 131, 152;
and choice, 152; and ownership,
22, 137; and property paradigms,
137–43
in vitro fertilisation (IVF), 3, 67–68
Iran, 103–4, 106
Israel, 66, 68, 77, 83, 88
Italy, 70

James, Henry, *The Spoils of Poynton*, 18
Jesudason, Sujatha, 95–96

Kant, Immanuel, 21, 22
Kantianism, 23, 116
kidneys: and body as object available for trade, 19; buyers of, 114,
117–18; commodification of, 107,
110–11; donors of, 4, 102, 172n9;
illicit harvesting of, 106; need for,
106; ownership of, 2; payment to
nonrelated donors for, 106; sale
of spare, 1; supply of, 4; and UK
Human Organ Transplant Act of
1989, 103
kidneys, market in, 16, 106–14; ban on,
103; benefits to human welfare of,
105; contingent features of, 113; and
debt, 109; desire to help others in,
109–10; exploitation in, 107, 113,
114; as illegal, 106–7; and intrusions
deep into body, 31; motivation
of providers of, 109; as reducing
choices, 145–46; and sense of self,
105; utilitarian perspective on, 105

labour, 4, 145; and bodily service,
82–83; and body, 9, 10, 30; choice
in, 90–91; and equality, 118–20;
freedom to sell, 19; gender inequality in, 91; and health and safety, 10;
as leasing out of capacities, 36; ownership of, 34–35, 36; as property,

36–37; and property in the person,
22; and property rights, 19; regulation of conditions of, 145, 146;
reproductive, 34–35, 81; requirements and risk exposure in, 86;
right to use, 97; safety requirements
in, 90–91; as separate entity, 36–37;
and skills and preferences, 12; social
division of, 12; and specialisations,
12, 120; as thing, 35; unpleasant, 118–19; for wages, 21–22; of
women, 35. *See also* employment
Lacey, Nicola, 45, 166n19
Lacks, Henrietta, 125, 126
land, 134
landlords, 130
landowners, 19
land tenure, communal, 121, 174n42
Lewis, Debra, 43–44, 52
Locke, John, 4, 20, 32, 34, 45, 128
Lukács, Georg, 22

MacKinnon, Catharine, 46
Marcus, Sharon, 55, 62
markets: banning of, 143–48; and
bodily tissues and parts, 149–50;
changes from, 153; and corruption,
7, 8, 9; as enabling specialisms, 115;
and equality, 7, 8, 12, 114–15; and
fairness, 7–8, 11–12; and payment
for services and donations, 151;
and property-objectification-
commodification-exploitation
chain, 104; and social understandings of worth, 149; and voluntary
choices, 7
market societies, 46
marriage, 2, 14, 18, 20, 79–80
Marx, Karl, 19
Marxism, 5, 21–22
McGregor, Joan, 54, 167n43
medical negligence, 128–29
medical research, 33–34, 98, 146–47.
See also research
medical science, 153

medical specimens, 14
medical technology, 3, 16–17, 153. *See also* biotechnology; reproductive technology
medical training, 98–99
medical treatment, 15
medical trials, 150
men: and blood donation vs. surrogacy, 101, 102; as defined by sexuality, 53; and inequality of prostitution, 140; pay for, 93; as protectors of women, 44; and rape, 42–44, 46, 57; surrogacy as affecting unequally, 91, 93, 102
military, 81
mind/body dualism, 5, 26, 27, 29, 53, 104, 105, 131
Moore, John, 33–34, 124–25, 126
Moore v. the Regents of the University of California, 33–34, 124–27
multiculturalism, 176n69
Munzer, Stephen, 40
Murphy, Jeffrie G., 168n48

Naffine, Ngaire, 20, 162n29
Nedelsky, Jennifer, 22–23, 55, 56, 131–32, 167n35
Nelkin, Dorothy, 98, 123, 128
New Jersey, 150
Nozick, Robert, 40
Nuffield Council on Bioethics, 138, 150, 151; *Human Bodies*, 148–49, 173n18
Nussbaum, Martha, 10, 23–24, 28, 30, 35

objectification: of body parts, 111–12; and commodification, 25–26, 104, 106, 107; and feminism, 27; literal, 23; metaphorical, 23; problems with, 18–19; and property claims, 104; recognition of humanity despite, 24; and sexuality as thing vs. activity, 55; total, 24; as treatment as thing, 23–24

O'Connell Davidson, Julia, 158n18
organ donation: and equality, 11; and gratitude of recipients, 116–17; and moral equality, 117–18; postmortem, 116; and presumed consent, 120–21; purpose of, 128; reciprocity in, 117; recompense for, 173n18; and research, 121. *See also* body parts
organ donors, 3–4; commercial exploitation of, 97; compensation for, 103–4, 116; insufficient numbers of, 154; motivation of, 116–17; payment to, 121, 150
organs: and agency, 8; desperate need for, 97; and equality, 11; right to sell, 97; trade in as illegal, 103. *See also* body parts
organ transplants: and medical technology, 17; payment for, 154
Overall, Christine, 72
ownership, 32, 123; as absolute right to control, 41; of body, 104; distinct and separable rights in, 129–30; and individual, 137; of labour, 34–35; and person as thing, 23–24; and rape, 54; rhetoric of, 20–23; and right to sell, 39–40; and self as distinct from capacities, 35–36; and use, 21

Paglia, Camille, 62
pain, 37–39, 54, 58, 61. *See also* vulnerability
Pande, Amrita, 69–70, 89
Pateman, Carole, 9, 22, 30, 35, 154, 157n5, 161n16
patriarchy, 8, 28, 79
Paul, St., 4
payment: and agency, 150; and blood donation, 93, 99–100, 138; for bodily services, 108; for body parts, 108, 148–52; of egg donors, 93–94, 150, 151; for embryos, 151; for gametes, 150–51; for kidneys, 106;

payment (*cont'd*)

    levels of, 108, 148; to organ donors, 121, 150; for organ transplants, 154; for surrogacy, 28, 70, 71, 72, 73, 74, 92–93, 94, 101, 148, 149–50, 154. *See also* compensation

Petchesky, Rosalind, 20, 40, 131

pharmaceutical companies, 124

physiotherapists, 31

Plaza, Monique, 50

poor people, 6, 99; and banning markets, 143–44; and body parts market, 7, 113, 114; normal human consideration for, 116; and surrogacy, 70, 87–88, 97

Posner, Richard, 49

pregnancy, 28, 81–82

property, 13–17, 31–41; absolute dominion over, 40; absolutist understanding of, 131–32; agency based understanding of, 32; as appropriately traded in market, 131; and autonomy, 55; bad as driving out good, 39–40; and body, 14, 37, 41, 65–66, 71, 105, 106, 128, 135, 136; and body parts market, 122–33; and boundaries and boundary crossing, 54–57; as bundle of relationships, 32; as bundle of rights, 34; as bundle of rights, powers, and claims, 32; and capitalism, 32; and commodification, 41, 123, 152; and commodity, 19–20; communal, 130; control rights to, 31, 32–33; defense of power of, 13; as despotic dominion, 31; disaggregated understanding of, 39; and embodied experience in rape, 54; and expression, 32; and Fabre, 122, 123; and feminism, 27; and Harris, 123; income rights to, 31, 32; and individualism, 134–55; and individual vs. society, 137–43; and inequality, 45, 136; inheritance of, 33; and intimate bodily services, 123–24; Kant on, 22; labour as,

36–37; and law, 39–40; as link to others, 32; and objectification-commodification-exploitation chain, 104, 106; owners of, 19–21; and personal control, 129; personal vs. fungible, 112; popular understandings of, 39–40, 131–32; and presumed consent, 121; private, 15, 20, 21, 32, 121, 129–30; as protecting, 14; as protection, 16; and public policy, 136–43; and rape, 2, 45, 46–49, 53–54, 63, 65, 152; and reciprocity, 39; as relationship between people, 32; and respect, 46; and Rousseau, 134; security of, 39; and self-alienation, 23; and self as distinct from capacities, 36; as self-mastery, 31; as shared, 39; and social convention, 135–36; as subject to our own choices and decisions, 131; theoretical vs. practical discourse about, 131; trespass on, 15; weak vs. strong rights of, 31; women as forms of, 43–44

property in the body, 124, 128–29, 131, 158n8; and bodily integrity, 15; and *Moore v. the Regents of the University of California*, 33–34; and rights for marginalized people, 33

property in the person, 34–35, 37, 124, 158n8; and Locke, 4; and self as distinct from capacities, 35–37; and self-ownership, 161n16; and subordination in labour, 22

property rights, 13–14, 32, 34, 37, 39–40, 105, 106, 136

prostitution, 1, 3, 16, 162n23; and body as incidental vs. whole point, 30; and body or self as property, 21; and choice, 8, 70; and coercion, 6; and commercial surrogacy, 66, 69, 157n5; and commodification, 70; contract for, 83; as contractual agreement, 69; and diverse relationships to sexuality, 139; and

recompense, 148, 173n18

Regina v. Kelly, 128

reimbursement, 148, 149, 151, 173n18.
  See also compensation; payment

reproductive technology, 3–4, 16–17,
  71

reproductive tourism, 151

research, 3, 14, 33–34, 35, 98, 105, 121,
  124–27, 134–35, 146–47

researchers, 132

Richards, Janet Radcliffe, 143

Roiphe, Katie, 62

Rose, Carol M., 13, 159n21

Rousseau, Jean-Jacques, 37, 134

Sandel, Michael, 9, 11, 75–76; *What
  Money Can't Buy*, 1, 7–8

Satz, Debra, 9, 80–81, 86, 91, 113, 114,
  139–40, 142, 146; *Why Some Things
  Should Not Be For Sale*, 1

Savulescu, Julian, 4, 105

Scheper-Hughes, Nancy, 118, 153

Schneider, Ingrid, 154; *Altruism Reconsidered*, 147

Schultz, Marjorie, 79, 84, 93

Scottish Highlands, land clearances
  in, 32

self: and bodily and sexual integrity,
  57; and body, 4, 30, 37, 112; and capacities, 35–37; and deep intrusions
  into body, 31; embodied, 30; as
  forfeited in contract pregnancy, 82;
  as minimised in ownership models
  of body, 104; as owner of body and
  capacities, 26; sense of, 2, 58, 105,
  111–13. *See also* identity

self-alienation, 22, 23. *See also*
  alienation

self-ownership, 69, 90; and bodily integrity, 38; and body parts market,
  123; and Cohen, 40–41, 164n58;
  and commodification, 26–27; definition of, 26–27; Kant's prohibition
  on, 22; in Marxism, 22; and mind/
  body dualisms, 29; and Naffine vs.

Cohen, 162n29; and Nozick, 40; and
  property in the person, 161n16; and
  property owners, 19–21; and rights
  of alienation and control, 129; and
  self-possession and self-control, 20;
  and surrogacy, 87

self-possession, 20, 38

sewage treatment plants, 159n21

sex: and commercial surrogacy, 67;
  as commodity, 47; and marriage,
  79–80; nonconsensual, 60–61; in
  prostitution, 70; and rape, 49, 52,
  58, 63; and sense of self, 58

sex trafficking, 6, 23

sexuality: diverse relationships to, 139;
  and identity, 9; and rape, 51–54,
  61; regulation of, 52; as thing vs.
  activity, 55; understandings of in
  rape, 60

sexual services: ban on sales of, 143–
  44; and body or self as property, 21;
  right to sell, 19

sex workers, 162n23; agency of, 6; motivation of, 138; property discourse
  rejected by, 65–66, 69; and rape, 57;
  and sexual preference and skill, 12.
  See also prostitution

Shalev, Carmel, 28, 79

Shanley, Mary, 82, 86, 90, 95–96

Silbaugh, Katherine, 27

slave owners, 40, 41, 129, 130

slavery, 2, 14, 23, 24, 83

social contract, 40

Southeast Asia, 68

Spain, 151

specialisation, 115, 119, 120

sperm: donation of, 93, 103, 132; market in, 105, 109

stem cell research, 3, 35, 98, 146–47.
  See also research

Stern, Elizabeth, 77, 78, 141, 170n25

Stern, Melissa, 170n25

Stern, William, 77, 78, 141

Stone, Lawrence, 69

Strathern, Marilyn, 165n9

surrogacy, 145; as alienation or diminution, 85; and blood donation, 101–2; choice of, 74–75; between close relatives and friends, 94, 95, 101; and commercialisation, 71; compensation for, 93–96, 101, 108, 109, 148, 149–50; consent in, 68, 76, 78, 92; distancing mechanisms in, 88; and diverse relationships to sexuality, 139; and equality, 12; and feminism, 27, 71; and gender inequality, 140; gestational, 67, 76–77, 85–86; global trade in, 12; in India, 12, 77, 83–84, 89, 168–69n2; and law, 68, 71; and market supply and demand, 94–95; and moral or civic duty, 93; motives for, 109; and natural vs. artificial pregnancy, 88; need for, 109; noncommercial, 148; payment for, 28, 70, 71, 94, 148, 149–50; precontract counselling services for, 141; and preferences, 12; reimbursement for expenses for, 92; as unequally affecting women vs. men, 91, 93, 102. *See also* commissioning parents; surrogates

surrogacy, altruistic, 3, 16, 71, 91–96; and commercial surrogacy, 70, 91–92, 93, 101

surrogacy, commercial, 16; and altruistic surrogacy, 70, 91–92, 93, 101; bans on, 91–92, 95; and body as property, 87; brokers for, 74, 75; and commodification, 70; as damaging, 96; distancing in, 87–91; and feminism, 28; and fungibility, 25; and law, 66–67; open model for, 88–89; payment for, 67, 68, 72, 73, 74, 93, 101, 154; and prostitution, 66, 69, 157n5; as purchase and sale of a reproductive service, 76; reference to gift of life in, 87; regulation of, 2; and renting of body, 68–70, 104; requirements, regulation and risk exposure in, 86, 87; and

self-ownership, 87; types of, 67; validity of, 84; and women, 66

surrogacy agencies, non-profit, 92

surrogacy contracts, 68, 69, 72, 73, 74; and awareness of surrogate's health and welfare, 110; enforceability of, 77–78, 80–91; as intrusive, 81; long-term commitment of, 81; requirements specified in, 83–84; and requirement to relinquish child, 78–79, 84–91; and woman's sense of identity, 81

surrogates: agency of, 76–80, 85; alienated pregnancy of, 82; as already having own children, 88; and altruism, 100–101; and body or self as property, 21; and children as use-value, 74, 75; child's knowledge of, 95–96; and choice and personal control, 97; commissioning parents' awareness of health and welfare of, 110; commissioning parents' relationship with, 88–89; consent of, 68, 76; decision to keep child by, 89; difficulty sustaining distance, 89; and economic necessity, 70, 97; emotions of, 100–101; equal protection for, 28; as genetic mother, 76, 77; and gift aspect, 97; happiness of, 85; insufficient numbers of, 154; joy of, 75; knowledge upon entering contract, 6, 8, 76–80, 96; as means to end, 110; payment of, 150; and prohibition on touch, 31; property discourse rejected by, 69–70; property rights of, 34–35; and refusal to surrender child, 76–80; for relatives or friends, 3; relinquishment of child by, 78–79, 84–91; and reproductive labour, 34–35; and right to choose, 69–70; as selling service, 73–74; surrender of child by, 72, 74

taxi driver, 36

Teman, Elly, 88

Thailand, 66, 91
Titmuss, Richard, 93, 94, 101, 102, 138; *The Gift Relationship*, 99, 100
Tober, Diane, 109
Tong, Rosemarie, 141

Ukraine, 66
United Kingdom, 4, 87–88, 89; blood donation in, 100, 101; and commercial vs. altruistic surrogacy, 91–93; Human Fertilisation and Embryo Authority (HFEA), 150–51; The Human Fertilisation and Embryology Act, 92; Human Organ Transplant Act, 103; noncommercial surrogacy industry in, 148; The Surrogacy Arrangements Act, 92; and surrogacy contracts, 77
United States, 66, 68; blood donation in, 100; commercial surrogacy industry in, 148; and commissioning parents' relationships with surrogates, 88–89; and gestational surrogates, 77; mandatory autopsy in, 120, 172n6; pay for egg donors in, 151; tissue banks in, 125
United States Uniform Commercial Code, 25
University of California, 33–34; Center for Reproductive Health, 128

vulnerability, 10, 11, 37, 64. *See also* pain

Wald, Alexandra, 46, 165n9
war, 24, 44
The Washington University v. Dr. W. Catalona et al., 127, 132
Wertheimer, Alan, 48, 50, 60–61, 168n48

West, Robin, 48, 63
West Africa, precolonial, 130
Whitehead, Mary Beth, 77, 78, 141, 170n25
Widdows, Heather, 143
Wilkinson, Stephen, 26, 110–11
Wolkowitz, Carol, 9, 158n18
women: abortion ban as affecting unequally, 102; agency of, 79; as baby machines, 91, 140; and blood donation vs. surrogacy, 101, 102; and body, 27–31; and choice in use of bodies, 84; as defined by sexuality, 52–53; equal protection for, 28; and family or community honour, 44; and feminism, 27; as forms of property, 43–44; and identity and sexual or reproductive capacities, 27; as independent vs. living with parents or husband, 43–44; and inequality of prostitution, 140; labour of, 35; low-skilled employment of, 53; and marriage, 14; and nonconsensual sex, 60–61; objectification of, 18–19; as Others, 29; as owners of sexual property, 44; pay for, 27, 28, 93, 145; as property holders, 46; and property in the person, 34–35; and property rights, 14; and prostitution, 66; and reproduction and identity, 9; reproductive labour of, 34–35; risks to, 35; and self-alienation, 23; status as sex objects, 53; and surrogacy, 66, 78–79, 91, 93, 102; as tainted by money and markets, 27
Woo-Suk, Hwang, 147
World Health Organization, 106

Yearworth & others v. North Bristol NHS Trust, 129, 130